A Guide To Father's Rights In New Jersey

Bari Zell Weinberger, Esq.

FAMILY LAW REFERENCE COLLECTION
Weinberger Divorce & Family Law Group

A Guide To Father's Rights In New Jersey

Table of Contents

4

About The Author

Bari Z. Weinberger, Esq. is a certified matrimonial law attorney and founding partner of Weinberger Divorce & Family Law Group of New Jersey. Ms. Weinberger has been named a Top Women in Law by New Jersey Law Journal and carries an AV Preeminent (highest) peer rating from Martindale Hubbell. She recently celebrated 10 years of recognition on the state's SuperLawyers list.

In addition to working with clients at her firm, Weinberger Divorce & Family Law Group, Ms. Weinberger is the Associate Author of the New Jersey Family Law Practice, 15th Ed., a 5-volume treatise utilized by virtually every family law judge and practitioner in the State of New Jersey.

www.WeinbergerLawGroup.com

Disclaimer

This book provides a general overview of New Jersey divorce and family law matters for informational purposes only. The contents included do not in any way supplement or replace legal advice obtained by a qualified and licensed attorney.

The information provided herein is based solely upon my professional experiences in the areas of New Jersey divorce and family law. While every effort has been made to ensure that the information contained in this book is helpful and of high quality, no representations or warranties of any kind are made with regard to the completeness or accuracy of the included content.

Please note that information provided within this guide is current as of publication date. Due to the complexity and frequency with which the divorce and family laws change, you should consult with a qualified attorney to determine the best course of action for your specific legal needs.

If you require legal advice based on the specifics of your case as it relates to New Jersey laws, please feel free to reach out to our office to schedule a consultation with one of our experienced attorneys. It would be our pleasure to help you.

For more information about other topics related to family law, such as alimony, domestic violence, prenuptial agreements, family mediation, child support, domestic partnerships, or any other family law related topics, please ask us about our other books. All guides in the series are designed, like this one, to help you to make sound decisions regarding your family's individual situation. Please keep in mind, however, that these books contain general information, and not legal advice. Always direct specific questions about your own situation to an attorney.

Weinberger Divorce & Family Law Group
Safeguarding Your Future™

Letter from the Author

When you're a dad going through divorce, I understand the concerns and fears you have about the custody process and whether it will honor your rights as a father and protect your relationships with your kids.

Fathers may feel like the deck is stacked against them in divorce, especially if conflict in their matter is running high or a full-blown custody battle is brewing. You want to know... what are the best strategies for safeguarding your kids? Can you get the parenting time you want with them? What are your rights if your ex is keeping your kids from you? Will the courts treat you fairly?

It is my goal that the book you hold in your hands gives you answers to all your most pressing questions *and* gives you peace of mind. Father's rights matter, and I hope this information empowers you to create a parenting and custody plan that will nurture and protect your kids and your relationships with them for years to come.

Something I think it is so important for dads in New Jersey to know up front is that all parenting and custody laws in New Jersey are gender neutral. There is nothing in the law that states mothers have more rights to children than fathers. In fact, in our modern court system, it is a core legal belief that it is in the child's best interests to spend quality time with each of their parents in as nearly an equal division of time as possible, whenever possible.

Gone are the days of the "tender years" doctrine when young children were thought to be better off with their mothers. With new understandings around child psychology and what children of divorce need to emotionally thrive, the courts now acknowledge that both parents are of equal importance to the child's development and long-term well-being.

Fathers now have more flexibility than ever to create the best parenting situation possible, and you will find this book filled with practical tips that can help you reach your custody goals - whatever those goals may be. As a reminder, the information provided in the book is for educational purposes only, so please work with a family law attorney to obtain individualized advice.

I would love to hear from you with any questions you have, or to schedule a free consultation with one of our father's rights attorney to begin safeguarding your rights. Drop me a line at bariw@wlg.com and let me know how we can be of help.

I wish you and your children all the very best!

Bari Z. Weinberger, Esq.

Chapter 1

Establishing Rights as a Father: New Jersey Paternity

Fathers sometimes face a threshold question regarding parenthood that mothers do not. New Jersey law generally presumes that a child's father is the husband of a child's mother at the time of the child's birth (or the mother's former husband, if the child was born within 10 months after a divorce or the husband's death).

If you were married to your child's mother during the applicable time frame, and no one has challenged your paternity, you probably need not concern yourself any further with this issue. You can skip directly to the next section, on "New Jersey Child Custody and Parenting Agreements." [1]

If you were not married to your child's mother, however, you must establish paternity some other way. Simply having your name on a child's birth certificate as the father is not sufficient. Both parents must also sign a voluntary acknowledgment of paternity. In New Jersey, this is called a Certificate of Parentage. The form is available at hospitals, local registrars, and county welfare agencies. Parents can complete it at any time up until a child's 23rd birthday. Once it is signed by both parents, notarized, and filed with the New Jersey Department of Health, it establishes legal paternity, unless the father rescinds it within 60 days. A challenge to paternity can then generally be based only on fraud, duress, or material mistake of fact.

Parents who are uncertain about the identity of a child's biological father can request a genetic test, known as a human leukocyte antigen (HLA) test, through their local county welfare agency. Genetic testing is simple, highly accurate, and costs only a few hundred dollars. In some cases, the cost may be covered by welfare. If the

------

[1] This book is written specifically for fathers. When we refer to a child's "other parent," this will usually mean the child's mother. We may also use the pronouns "she" or "her" because this person is most often a female. In some situations, however, the term "other parent" will refer not to a mother, but rather to a second father. When talking specifically about a parent of female gender, we will use the word "mother."

test results are positive, the agency will ask the mother and the identified father to sign a Certificate of Parentage.

A disagreement regarding paternity may also lead to an action in New Jersey Superior Court. Any of the following people or agencies can file a request for a paternity hearing:

- the child,

- the child's legal representative or guardian,

- the child's mother,

- a man claiming paternity, or

- a county welfare agency if the child is receiving state assistance.

If a child's alleged father denies paternity in court, the judge may order him to take the HLA test and attend a hearing. If paternity is conclusively established, the court will enter an Order of Paternity, which can be the basis for a child support request. A court can also issue a default paternity order if a man served with notice of the paternity hearing fails to appear.

Benefits in Determining Paternity

Most fathers want to be involved in their children's lives and welcome conclusive establishment of paternity. Others worry about the fact that a legal finding of paternity can lead to a court order for child support. Fathers who are hesitant to step up may change their minds when they understand that a legal finding of paternity is a necessary prerequisite to custody or visitation rights, including a father's right to have a say in decisions affecting his child's welfare. While fathers have much to gain from establishing legal parentage, those who gain the most are the children. Benefits to children may include:

- **Knowledge of Medical History:** Many medical conditions are hereditary. Knowing whether or not a biological father has a hereditary condition that could be passed on to the child could lead to early treatment, potentially forestalling serious complications down the road.
- **Eligibility for Medical Insurance:** A child may be eligible to receive medical benefits through a legal father's plan.
- **Eligibility for Government Benefits:** Some children may qualify for social security or veteran's benefits based on a legal father's disability or death.
- **Inheritance Rights:** If a child's legal father dies without a will, the child may stand to receive a portion of the father's estate during probate proceedings.
- **Emotional Security:** A healthy child-parent bond with two parents provides a child with added emotional security and sense of belonging. This can permeate many aspects of a child's life.

A New Jersey family law attorney can provide more information regarding the process and the potential effects of establishing paternity.

Paternity Rights of Non-Biological Fathers

Fathers who are not biological parents can gain full parental rights through adoption, or by following legal procedures if planning to have a child by means of assisted reproductive technology. In rare cases, fathers who are not legal parents can gain rights to custody or visitation through New Jersey's "psychological parent doctrine." All of these situations are briefly discussed below.

Adoptive Fathers

Current New Jersey law allows a child to have only two legal parents. One of the child's biological parents must therefore give up parental rights (either voluntarily or through a court action) before a non-biological father can gain them. This is true even if the would-be adoptive father is the child's step-parent and the child's legal parent approves of the adoption.

There are many avenues to adoption in New Jersey for both traditional and non-traditional fathers, including state adoption as well as domestic private adoption and international adoption. A full discussion of adoption law is beyond the scope of this book. You can find more information at the Weinberger Divorce & Family Law Group website. A family law attorney can also provide you with additional information.

Fatherhood and Assisted Reproductive Technology

Artificial Insemination and the Parentage Act

Under the New Jersey Parentage Act, a would-be father who opts to use donated sperm can be named as the legal father on a child's birth certificate provided that his wife, with the written consent of both spouses, is artificially inseminated under medical supervision. A recent amendment to the Act that became law as part of the New Jersey Gestational Carrier Agreement Act (further discussed below) clarifies that the medical supervision can be provided by a licensed physician, a physician assistant, or an advanced practice nurse. A man who donates sperm under medical supervision has no parental rights unless he has entered into a written agreement to the contrary with the child's mother.

The New Jersey Gestational Carrier Agreement Act

If a would-be father is the intended second father in a same-sex relationship and he and his partner are using a surrogate to become parents, then the biological parent who must relinquish rights will be the child's mother. For a heterosexual couple using a surrogate, the only parental right affected would be that of the intended mother, unless the couple is also using a sperm donor, in which case the information above would be applicable.

Second fathers often wish to establish parentage prior to a child's birth by means of a surrogacy contract. Until recently, this was possible only if a child was born outside of New Jersey, in a state recognizing surrogacy contracts. In New Jersey, such contracts were invalid. Even a surrogate with no genetic ties to a child gained legal parental status simply by giving birth to the child. She could not legally relinquish such rights until 72 hours after delivery, which meant that the second father had to wait until she did so, and then go through an adoption process.

This all changed on May 30, 2018, when Governor Murphy executed the New Jersey Gestational Carrier Agreement Act. The Act now allows a gestational surrogate to enter into a contract to bear a child by means of assisted reproductive technology for an intended parent or parents. The gestational carrier must waive any and all parental rights to the child, and the intended parent or parents must assume all responsibility and parentage of the child immediately upon its birth. New Jersey gestational carrier agreements are now binding upon all parties provided that they are executed in conformity with all requirements of the Act.

To enter into a valid agreement, a gestational surrogate (referred to as a "carrier") must be at least 21 years old, must have given birth previously, must pass medical and psychological evaluations, and must be represented by an independent attorney. The surrogate is permitted to recoup "reasonable expenses" from the intended parent(s). Such expenses are defined to include payments for medical care, an attorney, and counseling and living expenses during pregnancy and post-partum recovery.

The Act places requirements on intended parents as well. An intended parent must also complete a psychological evaluation and retain an independent attorney. If a court finds that a gestational carrier agreement is in compliance with the law, the judge will implement a pre-birth order of parentage in favor of the intended parents. Parentage then transfers immediately upon the child's birth, and the state registrar will issue a birth certificate naming the intended parent(s) as the legal parent(s) of the child.

Psychological Fathers

If you are not a child's legal father, but you have acted as the child's father for a significant period of time with the approval of a legal parent, there is a possibility that you may have custody or visitation rights under the "psychological parent" or "de facto parent" doctrine. New Jersey law considers third parties who have demonstrated all the required elements of a psychological parent to stand "in parity" - that is, on equal ground - with a biological or adoptive parent in a custody case. This means that a court will resolve custody and visitation disputes between legal and psychological parents by analyzing the best interests of the child according to the same factors that would apply to a custody dispute between two legal parents. We will discuss these "best interests" factors in depth later in this book.

New Jersey courts have determined that a third party may have a psychological parent claim even when a child already has two fully involved legal parents. This kind of claim is not easy to prove, however. It requires the following four elements:

- the biological or adoptive parent consented to, and encouraged, the third party's formation of a parent-like relationship with the child;

- the third party and the child lived together in the same household;

- the third party assumed significant responsibility for the child's care, education and development, including contributing toward the child's support (financial or otherwise) without any expectation of compensation; and

- the third party functioned in a parental role for long enough to establish a bonded, dependent, parent-child type of relationship.

The rights of psychological parents in New Jersey are limited to custody and visitation and will ordinarily end when a child reaches majority. A court can grant any variation of legal or physical custody and parenting time, but this does not give the psychological parent other rights. So, for example, if another third party, such as a child's grandparent, is requesting visitation with a child, the psychological parent does not begin with any presumption of elevated status. A grandparent requesting visitation over the objection of a legal parent has to prove that denying such visitation would result in harm to the child. A grandparent requesting visitation over the objections of a psychological parent, however, would have no such burden. Instead the court would simply analyze the situation according to the best interests of the child.

In New Jersey, there is also no automatic responsibility for a psychological parent to pay child support. The court will normally look only to the legal parents when ordering support. Nevertheless, a psychological parent who voluntarily contributes to a child's financial support cannot arbitrarily stop doing so if that would cause the child to suffer financial harm.

Case Studies: Establishing Parental Rights -
A Legal Father and a Psychological Step-Father

When Tyler met Amanda, her son Jason was almost two years old. Amanda had been in a relationship with Jason's father, Karl, while she was studying in Germany. She returned to the United States before Jason was born, and Karl stayed behind. Karl acknowledged Jason as his son and visited him in New Jersey both right after he was born and for several weeks during the following summer. After that, Karl continued to send gifts and small amounts of money for the baby, but he and Amanda did not enter into any kind of formal custody or child support arrangement.

Tyler and Amanda soon began to spend a lot of time together, both as a couple and as a family unit with Jason. After about a year of dating, they married. During the marriage, Tyler acted as Jason's father in every way, participating fully in all child care responsibilities. As Jason grew older, Tyler took him to extracurricular activities and even acted as his youth hockey coach. Although Karl continued to stay in contact with Jason and visited him for several weeks nearly every summer over the next few years, it was always Tyler who provided the bulk of Jason's financial support. Jason called Tyler "Daddy;" Karl was "Papa Karl."

After about six years, Amanda filed for divorce, and she and Jason moved out of the family home. She told Tyler that she wanted him to stay in Jason's life, but she didn't want to enter into a custody or visitation agreement. After all, she said, Jason already had a legal father who wanted to stay in his life. She suggested that Tyler and Jason spend an afternoon together a couple of times a month. Tyler was heartbroken. He considered Jason to be his son, and could not imagine having so little contact with him.

Tyler contacted Lauren Haas, a family law attorney, who advised him that although he had no legal rights as a father, he might qualify as a "psychological parent." If so, she said, this would allow him to ask the court for more parenting time. Attorney Haas felt that Tyler had a strong case, since he had clearly assumed the role of a parent to Jason with Amanda's full approval, and they had all lived together as a family for more than six years. If Tyler succeeded in his claim, Ms. Haas explained, he would have the same custody and visitation rights as a legal parent. Then, if he and Amanda couldn't work out a satisfactory parenting plan, a court would decide whether or not spending more time with Tyler would be in Jason's best interests. Attorney Haas also advised Tyler that he might be responsible for paying child support, since he had been voluntarily supporting Jason financially.

Tyler told Amanda what the attorney had said and also assured her that he was perfectly willing to pay child support. After Amanda consulted with her own attorney, Amanda, Tyler, and Karl eventually reached an agreement together without anyone going to court. They all signed the agreement and then filed it in New Jersey family court to ensure that it would be enforceable.

Under their agreement, all three parties shared legal custody of Jason, but Amanda had "final say" over certain specified matters. Amanda was also designated as Jason's primary residential parent. Karl, who had since married and had another child, wanted only a guarantee of up to four consecutive weeks of parenting time during the summers, along with ongoing access to communication with Jason throughout the year. Now that Jason was getting older, Karl also wanted up to half of his visits to take place in Germany. During Jason's first overseas trip, both Kristin and Tyler would be welcome to come along for the first week. After that, Karl would ensure that they both had daily access to Jason via telephone or Skype. Karl would pay for all of Jason's transportation expenses, as well as all of his basic needs during visitation periods.

Kristin and Tyler would each have up to two consecutive weeks of vacation time with Jason during the summers. During the school year, Jason would live primarily with Kristin, but he would stay with Tyler for three nights every other weekend, from 6:00 p.m. on Friday until the start of school on Monday. He would also have dinner with Tyler every other Thursday or Friday during the weeks they were not spending the weekend together. Tyler would continue to participate fully as a parent, attending school conferences and extracurricular activities and coaching Jason's hockey teams. Tyler agreed to pay child support according to a calculation that he and Amanda worked out under the Child Support Guidelines.

Chapter 2: New Jersey Child Custody and Parenting Agreements

The most important thing that fathers need to understand about laws governing child custody and visitation in the State of New Jersey is that such laws are gender neutral. Both parents begin with equal rights. The law also begins with a presumption that children benefit from frequent and continuing contact with both parents. As we will discuss in further detail below, fathers can therefore begin negotiations in a child custody dispute knowing that, unless some special circumstance exists, liberal visitation is the minimum they can expect to achieve.

Fathers who share parenting duties equally before a separation or divorce generally have a good case for equal or nearly equal parenting time. Fathers who have acted as primary caretakers generally have a good case for primary physical custody.

While courts once believed that mothers were better natural caretakers for very young children, this has not been true for many years. In the past, a legal stance known as the "tender years doctrine" sometimes severely impacted fathers who wanted primary or shared custody of children six years old or younger. The doctrine was based on a belief that young children needed to be with their mothers for the vast majority of the time in order to prevent damage to this primary attachment bond. Research in child development, however, has not strongly supported this idea, and instead tends to show that even very young children can form strong bonds with multiple caregivers, provided that they spend frequent periods of time with them.

The incorporation of gender neutral policies into the law reflects a recognition by the courts and the legislature that the tender years doctrine resulted in unjustified prejudice against fathers. As further discussed below, children do have varying needs at different ages, and these needs should be addressed with flexible and evolving parenting plans. As a father, however, you can be confident that your role is not peripheral; it is critical to your child's happiness and positive development.

Some fathers fear that even though custody law is now gender-neutral, judges will not honor this neutrality in practice due to long-entrenched and prejudicial attitudes favoring mothers. The reality is however, that fathers who persist in claiming their rightful roles as equal parents and in making their case to both the other parent and the judge (if it comes to that) are very likely to end up with a fair parenting agreement. Mothers are still awarded primary physical custody somewhat more often than fathers are, but this is mainly because mothers are still somewhat more likely to act as primary parents. Courts favor changing existing arrangements as little as possible when parents separate, to avoid adding additional stress to children whose lives are already in upheaval. A second reason that mothers are more likely to receive primary custody than fathers are, is that mothers are simply more likely to ask for it. Many fathers are unaware that they have equal rights when it comes to custody. Fathers who negotiate for primary or joint custody in mediation or argue for it in court are often successful.

Ultimately, courts decide custody and visitation matters according to the best interests of the children involved. As a father, you must carefully consider how those needs interact with your own availability and your other life responsibilities. As a general premise, however, no father who wants to be an active parent should settle for a plan affording him only minimal contact with his children.

Structuring New Jersey Child Custody

The next most important thing for fathers to know when thinking about custody arrangements, is that courts in New Jersey urge parents, whenever possible, to make their own decisions regarding how they will share parenting responsibilities and time. Even if you feel that you and your child's other parent are not on the same page, you will usually be better off trying to come up with a mutually agreeable solution. In most cases, parents have the best knowledge about their children's development and unique needs. Judges lack both the necessary time and the personal knowledge about individual families that would permit them to make the best decisions. The ultimate test of any parenting plan will be whether or not it meets the best interests of the children, but courts afford parents every opportunity to create a plan that will work for their entire restructured family.

New Jersey parents have a lot of flexibility in designing parenting plans. It's important to consider that any plan has two separate components:

Physical Custody

Physical custody - also known as "residential custody" - governs a child's physical location. One parent or the other has physical custody of a child at all times, including the time that the child is in school or is engaging in extracurricular activities. If one parent has "sole physical custody" this generally means that the child is living with a custodial parent the majority of the time, while the non-custodial parent has visitation time that is less than the equivalent of two overnight periods per week, not including vacation and holiday time. "Shared physical custody" or "shared parenting time," by contrast, generally refers to an arrangement where a child spends the equivalent of more than two overnight periods per week with each parent. This includes arrangements where a child alternates blocks of time with each parent, such as three days with one parent and four with the other, or one week at a time with each parent.

Legal Custody

A parent with legal custody has the authority to participate in major decisions regarding a child's health, education, and general welfare. This includes such things as where a child will attend school, what kind of religious upbringing a child will have, and when a child requires medical treatment beyond routine care or emergency treatment. A parent with sole legal custody can make all such major decisions for the child without consulting the other parent. Parents with joint legal custody must work together to make decisions.

Parents can agree to joint legal custody without necessarily having each parent participate equally in all major decisions. It can sometimes be smoother to assign one parent or the other as a tie-breaker around specific aspects of a child's life. For example, one parent may have the authority to override the other in decisions regarding religious upbringing while the other has the final say over educational decisions. While this type of split authority is less common than simple joint legal custody, it can occasionally be the best solution.

Combining Custody Options in Parenting Plans

Beyond the policy in favor of shared parental responsibility and frequent contact with both parents, New Jersey law does not favor any particular custody arrangement. Courts have authority to divide physical and legal custody between parents in any combination. The following are the most common types of arrangements:

- **Joint Legal Custody with a Parent of Primary Residence (PPR).** Joint legal custody is very common. It tends to be acceptable to both parents, as it allows both of them to participate actively in their children's lives. Parents share decision-making authority over major health, education and general welfare issues, while the parent who is with a child at any given time makes day-to-day decisions in the child's best interests and notifies the other parent as appropriate. In most parenting plans where parents have joint legal custody, the child nevertheless lives with a custodial parent, or "Parent of Primary Residence" (PPR), the majority of the time. The non-custodial parent, or "Parent of Alternate Residence" (PAR), typically has a more traditional visitation schedule, such as alternating weekends. If the parents live fairly close together, the PAR often has a mid-week activity with the child as well. The terms "Parent of Primary Residence" and Parent of Alternate Residence" are used in the child support guidelines and are relevant to dividing responsibility for financial support between the parents. We will discuss child support in depth later in this book.

- **Shared Legal and Physical Custody.** If the child spends more than the equivalent of about two overnight periods per week (not including vacation and holiday time) with each parent, the arrangement might be considered shared physical and legal custody. Although many parents would like to share time equally or nearly equally, this type of arrangement requires a high degree of communication and coordinated co-parenting. For that reason, fewer parents are successful with it over the long-term. A spirit of cooperation, however, combined with creative scheduling, can often make shared custody work. There are many possible scheduling variations, including alternating weeks or alternating shorter blocks of time. As will be discussed later in this book, the distinction between joint legal custody and shared legal and physical custody may be important for child support calculations.

- **Sole Legal and Physical Custody.** A parent with sole legal and physical custody is the residential custodian for the child and is also responsible for all major decisions regarding the child's health, education, and welfare. The parent is not required to consult with or notify the non-custodial parent. Although some parents agree to this type of arrangement for practical reasons, in the majority of cases, it is the result of a court determination that one parent is absent or unfit due to circumstances such as a history of child abuse or neglect, or drug addiction. In most such cases, the non-custodial parent will still have visitation with the child, but the visitation may be supervised or restricted to ensure the child's safety.

Finding the Best Custody Option

Whatever your parenting plan eventually looks like, it should take into account all of the practical considerations facing your family, including children's school requirements and extracurricular activities, parents' work schedules, child care needs, any planned travel, the location and involvement of extended family members, children's current ages and developmental levels, planning for future changes, and any other circumstances affecting your family.

Parents caught up in negotiating plans may find that there are multiple options that will address the best interests of their children. This leaves many wondering how to decide which option is truly best. A common question is whether it is better for children to split time equally between homes or better for them to spend most of their time at one primary home. Unfortunately, there is no simple answer to this question. The best option for each family will depend on consideration of all of the circumstances. Child development experts do generally agree that in most cases children will do best when they have close relationships with both parents. A parent can be fully involved in parenting, however, without having equal physical time with a child.

Positive Effects of Consistency

Child development experts strongly agree that consistency is important for children. Children experiencing parental separation or divorce face many changes. Parents who have divided parenting tasks in a certain way for a considerable amount of time will generally find that duplicating these pre-existing arrangements as closely as possible will provide children with the greatest possible stability. Parents can also minimize the impact of necessary or desirable changes to the "status quo" by implementing such changes in a gradual and structured manner.

If you are a father facing changes to your parental role, you may find this stressful. It is important to be patient and remember that children find such disruptions stressful as well. The entire family is likely to go through a somewhat bumpy adjustment period. When children react negatively to changes, hardworking parents can find themselves worn down. You may find it challenging to insist that children adhere to a new parenting schedule. Enforcing the schedule can be easier with younger children who are more portable, but younger children may also become more visibly upset. Commitment and close attention to children's individual needs can ease all of you through this difficult transition.

Developmental Concerns

Parents should be aware that children's needs change with age. While stability is important, parenting plans usually need to be modified and adapted as children grow. A good parenting plan will take age-related developmental needs into account. If you have questions or concerns about your child's developmental needs, you may wish to consult with a child development expert, such as a psychologist or a family therapist experienced in working with restructuring families. The following are a few basic age-based considerations to keep in mind:

- **Infants**. Children who are younger than about five generally bond more easily with caregivers when they do not spend long periods of time away from them. As a general rule, the younger the child, the shorter the gaps between visits with either parent should be in order to foster optimal bonding with both parents. Infants can pose special challenges, not only because they require the shortest time spans between visits, but also because scheduling visits requires accommodating sleeping and feeding schedules. Newborns often nurse virtually around the clock while sleeping only in short bursts. They take varying amounts of time to settle into more predictable feeding and sleeping schedules. Some nursing mothers have great success with pumping milk for a father to use during parenting time, while other mothers find this to be difficult or impossible. A schedule providing for frequent but relatively brief visits may be taxing for the parents but best for the child. The best parenting schedules for infants build in frequent modifications to keep pace with the child's rapidly changing development.

- **Preschool Children**. Children who are at least preschool age (three or four years old) may be able to tolerate schedules that require the child to alternate blocks of several days at a time with each parent. Once a child is closer to school age (about five or six years old) parents can try schedules that require longer gaps, such as alternating weekends or entire weeks. If parents of very young children want to work toward a schedule that includes longer gaps, they can build gradual modifications into the plan. Confronting these issues before they occur can ease stress and prevent the need to constantly renegotiate plans or engage in on-going litigation.

- **Older Children**. By the time a child reaches school age, the success or failure of different schedules depends more on the child's individual temperament and out-of-home commitments than on general developmental needs. Some children happily switch from home to home while others do better with one primary home base. If you want your child to split time between homes, but your child is very sensitive to being out of familiar surroundings, you may be able to address this by duplicating the environment in each home as closely as possible. Duplicating items can be expensive, of course, and not every family is equipped to do this. If you find that this is not feasible for your family, and that one primary home is more practical, do not assume that your bond with your child will suffer if you are not the primary parent. Child development experts generally agree that once children are past preschool age, maintaining strong parent-child bonds depends less on the amount of physical time a child spends with a parent than on the parent's commitment and ongoing efforts to stay engaged. Parents with less physical time can use phone calls or social media options to stay in close contact.

- **Teenagers**. As children approach adolescence, they may simply refuse to comply with a schedule that does not fit well with the demands of their many activities and their often busy social lives. Parents of older children and teenagers will generally have an easier time if they allow them to have an increasing amount of input into parenting arrangements. Failing to address a child's increasing autonomy needs can set the stage for difficult power struggles down the line.

Pros and Cons of Common Parenting Plans

Traditional Parenting Plans (Joint Legal Custody with a PPR)

A more traditional parenting schedule, in which children spend most of their time in one parent's household, usually works well when one parent has taken on the primary parenting role before separation or divorce. This often happens because the other parent has a more demanding work schedule. In the past, the parent with the more demanding schedule was usually the father, but this is no longer necessarily true. Both mothers and fathers now commonly act as primary caretakers both before and after divorce.

A more traditional schedule also tends to work well for children who need a more consistent environment and do not tolerate change well. As noted above, parents who want to divide time more equally may be able to accommodate such children by duplicating home environments as closely as possible, but this will generally take more effort and be more expensive. Another option is to start off with a traditional schedule and build in changes gradually.

One drawback of a traditional parenting arrangement after divorce is that it may limit the ability of the parent acting as primary caretaker to accept certain types of employment. This issue can become more important after divorce because of the greater cost of maintaining two separate households as opposed to one. Even if the higher earner can absorb the increased costs, the primary caretaker may find that divorce inspires a desire to work on developing as career outside the home. In either case, parents may want to start out maintaining a traditional schedule to minimize drastic changes in parental roles, but then build some changes in over time that will make it easier for the primary parent to find appropriate and fulfilling work.

Another potential risk with a traditional schedule is that the non-custodial parent will be less involved in routine parenting activities and may slip into more of a babysitter's role. Non-custodial parents can guard against this risk by adopting new routines like regular nightly phone-checks or on-line chats with children. If you end up being the parent with less physical time, be sure to build these options into your parenting agreement as part of the plan. A scheduled call with your child every night at 8 p.m., for example, can become a comforting ritual for your child to depend on.

<u>Equal-Time Parenting Plans (Shared Legal and Physical Custody)</u>

Many fathers are interested in equal parenting time. When this kind of arrangement works well, it can provide the best of both worlds, allowing each parent frequent and ongoing contact with children. As previously noted, however, for equal time sharing to be successful, both parents must maintain a high commitment to close co-parenting. There are also practical requirements. Parents need to live relatively close to one another. There must be enough money to go around, so that each parent can maintain sufficient full-time living space for children. Children will generally need to keep more belongings at each home to prevent frequent trips back and forth. A flexible and collaborative attitude by all involved is essential. Parents must be able to work together, and must be committed to addressing problems as they come up.

If you have long been a committed primary parent or an equal co-parent, you may find it relatively easy to adapt to shared parenting. If, on the other hand, you have relied mainly on your spouse to address children's needs while you pursued other goals, you may be in for a shock—at least initially. Shared parenting can impact all aspects of life. While it tends to be less-burdensome on a parent who would otherwise have primary custody, it can seriously impact the work options and schedules of both parents. Being available full-time for alternate weeks or half-weeks is a considerable responsibility. If you are in the process of considering an equal time-sharing arrangement, carefully map out options on daily, weekly, and monthly calendars before finalizing your agreement. You can refer to the checklist of parenting responsibilities that appears in "Preparing for Court: Keeping Good Records," later in this book, to help you plan.

Things to Include in Your Parenting Plan

Regardless of what type of custody option you choose, there are certain items you should be sure to include in your parenting plan. New Jersey parenting plans must designate the child's primary residence. They also must describe how parents will share decision making on major issues such as education, medical and dental treatment, and religious upbringing. A plan should also include a specific schedule addressing how the parents will share time with the children.

Parents who are less amicable may benefit from a detailed calendar that specifies exactly when a child is with each parent. This type of specificity results in a more enforceable plan. For example, a plan stating that parents will alternate weekends provides no support for a father trying to prove that the kids should be with him on any particular weekend. A plan stating that one parent has a child on the first and third weekends of every month, on the other hand, does provide such support.

The downside to a highly specific plan can be a loss of flexibility. Parents with this kind of plan should get a note from the other parent confirming any one-time changes, just in case issues come up later. Parents who are better at collaborative co-parenting and are willing to juggle things around fairly casually, and who also have children that can handle frequent changes, may want to keep things more general. Some parents specify only that they will divide time in a certain percentage during a normal week, or that they will each have a certain number of overnights each week. They agree between themselves on how this will usually work, but do not set it in stone by including it in the parenting plan.

Even parents who wish to keep things flexible often benefit from more specificity regarding division of holidays, birthdays, and vacations, as these tend to be occasions that generate higher emotions. Some parents alternate holidays, while others who live close to one another decide to divide up time on each holiday. If you have questions about how specific your plan needs to be, talk to an attorney.

In addition to spelling out details of time-sharing, parents may want to address the following:

- access to children's medical records, report cards teachers, etc.,
- first rights of refusal for babysitting,
- responsibility for specific expenses and sharing of unanticipated expenses,
- responsibility for transportation of children and transportation costs,
- responsibility for taking off work if necessary to care for a sick child,
- addressing potential schedule changes
- modifying plans as children get older,
- possible attendance at mediation to resolve conflicts over the plan or joint decisions in the future, and
- any other agreements parents wish to include.

Case Studies: New Jersey Child Custody and Parenting Agreements

1.   Shared Legal & Physical Custody between Father and Mother:

Travis and Kristin were married for seven years. When they made the difficult decision to divorce, they had three children, Joshua, who was five years old, Olivia, who was almost three, and Lyla, who was just 9 months. Both Travis and Kristin had pursued full-time careers since before they were married. Both had also been hands-on parents since their children were born. At the time of the divorce, Joshua was in kindergarten. He also went to day care both before and after school, to allow Travis and Kristin enough time to commute back and forth to Manhattan. Olivia attended the same day care facility full-time. Kristin's mother currently watched baby Lyla during the day, but the plan was for Lyla to start going to day care part-time when she turned a year old, and full-time starting at age two.

Both Kristin and Travis had worked hard to build a routine that allowed them to develop ambitious careers while also meeting their children's needs. The parents divided child care responsibilities as equally as possible. On week days, they typically dropped the children off at day care together in the morning and also picked them up together on the way home. In the mornings, Travis got the kids dressed and ready while Kristin packed lunches and snacks and stocked the diaper bag and backpacks. In the evenings, they took turns cooking dinner and overseeing bath time, teeth brushing and pajamas. They also took turns reading the children bedtime stories. If a child was sick, the parents would alternate taking time off from work.

They treated weekends as time for the whole family to be together and participate in fun activities.

In spite of the success of their egalitarian parenting arrangement, Kristin believed that having one primary custodial parent and one primary home after the divorce would provide the children with greater consistency. She wanted the kids to live with her during the week and spend only alternate weekends with Travis. Travis, however, was not happy about the prospect of being relegated to weekend dad. He proposed that they alternate full weeks. The court sent Travis and Kristin to mandatory parenting mediation. When they failed to reach an agreement that satisfied both of them, they agreed to hire a joint expert to perform a "best interests" custody evaluation.

The expert, a forensic psychologist named Dr. Gordon, concluded that neither Kristin's proposal nor Travis's adequately addressed the current best interests of Joshua, Olivia and Lyla. Kristin's proposal would deprive them of the day-to-day care they were accustomed to getting from their father. Travis's proposal, on the other hand, would take both parents away from the children for blocks of time that were too long to be developmentally appropriate for such young children, particularly for Olivia and Lyla.

Dr. Gordon believed that the kids would have the best chance of continuing to form and maintain strong bonds with each parent if they were able to see each of them on a regular basis without long absences in between. He recommended a 2-2-3 schedule. Every other week, the children would spend Monday and Tuesday nights with Travis, Wednesday and Thursday nights with Kristin, and then Friday through Sunday nights back with Travis. On the alternate weeks, the schedule would flip; Kristin would have the children for Monday and Tuesday, Travis for

Wednesday and Thursday, and Kristin for Friday through Sunday. Dr. Gordon also noted that building in a 30 minute Skype call each evening with the parent the children were not currently with would help duplicate their current routine as closely as practically possible.

Dr. Gordon acknowledged that for many parents, the amount of switching from home to home necessitated by a 2-2-3 schedule was quite challenging. If Travis and Kristin found this to be the case, then once Lyla was at least two years old, they could consider a 2-2-5-5 schedule. The children would then spend Mondays and Tuesdays with one parent, Wednesdays and Thursdays with the other, and alternate three day weekends with each parent. This schedule would extend the longest alternating blocks of time from three days to five days (Wednesdays through Sundays for one parent, and Fridays through Tuesdays for the other). If they eventually wanted to alternate full weeks, Dr. Gordon recommended that they wait until Lyla was entering kindergarten.

The court adopted Dr. Gordon's recommendations and ordered a 2-2-3 parenting schedule. The judge also urged the parents to maintain flexibility over time, and to work out any future changes by mutual agreement or through mediation.

2. Father's Involvement in a Parenting Plan for an Infant:

Jessica, 32, and Michael, 26, were together as a couple for only a few months before Jessica unexpectedly became pregnant. Although she thought the relationship with Michael was unlikely to last, Jessica had always wanted children, so she decided to keep the baby. Sure enough, the couple began to drift apart before Jessica even told Michael about the pregnancy. When she did tell him, he was shocked. He told her he wasn't ready to be a father, and for the next couple of weeks, he tried to talk her into terminating the pregnancy. Jessica told him there was no way she was doing that, but that he needn't worry about being involved with the child. She was fully committed to making do as a single mother.

Much to Michael's surprise, over the next few months he became increasingly disturbed at the thought of his child existing in the world without him. Shortly before Jessica gave birth to a healthy baby boy named Noah, Michael told her that he'd had a change of heart. He wanted to participate fully as a father and support his child. Jessica was surprised, and she was also not entirely sure she was happy about Michael's new decision. She had concluded that he was too immature to be a reliable father, and that it might be better for her and Noah to be on their own.

Michael contacted a family law attorney to help him decide what to do. The attorney explained that New Jersey law starts with the assumption that it is generally best for children to have two involved parents. She gave Michael some information about parent-child bonding, and some sample parenting plans.

Michael shared everything the attorney had said and all the materials he had received with Jessica. He also told her that he was planning to take a parenting class and learn CPR so that she would feel more comfortable about leaving him alone with the baby. Slowly, Jessica began to realize that it would be a positive thing for Noah to have a father in his life. She and Michael began to talk extensively about what kind of plan they could build that would work for both of them and also be best for Noah.

Because they went to great lengths to educate themselves, both new parents understood that as an infant, Noah would need to spend short and frequent periods of time with each of them to meet his early bonding needs. They also knew that they would need to adjust the schedule several times over time, both to make things easier for them and to keep pace with Noah's developmental needs. They spent several hours talking about different ways that they could structure things. Eventually they agreed to try the following:

Michael would start out by visiting Noah three times a week, for three to five hours at a time. After about six months, he would extend at least one of the weekly visitation periods to about eight hours. When Noah was between nine months and a year old, Michael would have one overnight visit per week, while keeping the other two weekly visits at about six to eight hours each. If everything went well, once Noah was between one and a half and two years old, he would be able to spend every other weekend per month with Michael. They would also keep the single overnights on the alternate weeks, plus at least one of the six to eight hour visits each week.

Michael and Jessica were fortunate to live very close to one another, making the short but frequent visits feasible for both of them. They agreed to revisit their parenting plan when Noah turned three. At that point, they believed they would be able to work out a plan that could remain stable for at least a few years. In the meantime, they both agreed to do their best to co-parent cooperatively to meet Noah's needs.

At the urging of his attorney, Michael asked Jessica to sign a written parenting agreement so that he could file it in family court. He also asked that the agreement specify joint legal custody. At first Jessica resisted this. She was still concerned about Michael's maturity and did not want to have to share major decision-making with him. After they implemented their time-sharing plan and followed it for several months, however, Jessica could see for herself how dedicated Michael was to participating fully as a parent. She then agreed to joint legal custody. She contacted her own attorney to review the parenting agreement Michael's attorney had drafted, and after working out a few minor disagreements, they were able to finalize the agreement and file it in court without a legal battle.

Chapter 3

Reaching Out-of-Court Agreements

At the most basic level, demonstrating a sincere desire to be an equally involved parent, and a willingness to conduct your life in a way that will put the best interests of your children first, will give you the best chance of maximizing time with your children. The first person you may need to convince regarding your intentions may well be your child's other parent. If the two of you can work out a mutually agreeable schedule out-of-court, you can avoid a great deal of conflict. You can also grant your children the gift of two parents who are able to work together on their behalf.

Resolving custody disputes between yourselves, with the assistance of a mediator if necessary, is almost always easier and far less expensive than engaging in a costly and unpleasant court battle. Nevertheless, in some cases, a court battle is inevitable. Even if things seem to be going well initially, it is worth taking certain steps early in the process to prepare for the possibility of such a battle. There are some tips regarding appropriate cautionary steps later in this book. In the meantime, paying attention to the following considerations may help you succeed without going to court.

Keep An Open Mind and Cultivate Compassion

Custody issues are especially likely to generate high conflict due to the deep emotional bonds parents form with their children. Working out parenting plans may require resolving emotionally wrenching dilemmas involving lifestyles choices and career trajectories. Many fathers, for example, struggle with the difficulty of maintaining a stable career path while also taking on a greater role as a parent. Even fathers who are already successfully balancing equal parenting responsibilities and work commitments must confront the reality that it can be much more expensive to maintain two homes as opposed to one.

Fear and anger are natural reactions when confronting such dilemmas. Some fathers also become angry because they believe (sometimes rightly and sometimes not) that the other parent is intentionally trying to marginalize them. If you find yourself feeling unfairly judged, it is critical to refrain from becoming reactive. Try to get to the heart of the other parent's concerns. Be especially sensitive to any safety concerns, as these are often "hot buttons" that can spike fear and irrationality if not fully addressed. If you find tensions escalating, strive to maintain an open mind and a willingness to compromise. Remember that the other parent, just like you, is undoubtedly struggling with deep emotional issues. Listen with compassion and understanding. Not only can such an attitude ease the stress that tends to breed anger and resentment, it can facilitate a more rapid resolution.

Keep in mind that the way you present your arguments can help preserve your co-parenting relationship and keep you out of court: Always focus on the best interests of your children. If you emphasize your true desire to be helpful and propose taking on a greater share of some of the less pleasant responsibilities of parenting in exchange for more time participating in the enjoyable aspects, you may succeed in building up more goodwill than you initially thought possible.

If both you and the other parent have a history of substantial participation in child care, and both of you want primary custody, then you are going to have to decide how closely you are willing and able to work together for the sake of your children. An equal time sharing plan is often a good compromise, but it is not always a realistic goal. It can be especially challenging for parents who are willing to share time equally to realize that this might not be feasible on a practical level simply because they live a considerable distance apart. Sometimes children's schooling or extracurricular needs are the most important factor. Sometimes children's unique temperamental or developmental needs take priority. Good parenting plans will take all such factors into account.

Consider Private Mediation
If you are not having much success reaching agreement on a parenting plan, but you are still committed to keeping your disagreements out of court and preserving

your family's privacy, you can consider using a private mediator to help resolve your parenting issues. Mediation has many benefits including confidentiality. Parents embroiled in custody disputes often view disagreements as win-lose battles. Fear and reactivity can contribute to a tendency to lash out and attack the other parent. When such disputes are aired in court, the result may be a public record that shows the worst of each parent. Private mediation can dramatically reduce conflict in the family while also preventing creation of a public record. It can be pursued either before or after filing a court case.

Mediation is especially appropriate for addressing parenting disputes because of the detrimental effect high conflict scenarios tend to have on children. Children who are able to see their parents come together in an effort to improve things for everyone in the family feel more secure. Parents who choose to mediate have the opportunity to express their deepest feelings and their positive wishes for their children to each other. They also learn that the possibilities for creative parenting plans that address the needs of everyone in the family are virtually endless. The presence of a neutral party to guide discussions keeps parents focused on flexible and collaborative problem-solving. You can find more information on mediation at Weinberger Law Group's Mediation Center.

High Conflict Parenting

If your co-parenting relationship is so contentious that even private mediation is fruitless, then for the sake of your children, you will need to find other ways to defuse the situation. Child development experts overwhelmingly agree that conflict-filled environments impact children negatively. Research shows that conflict in the family affects children more than parental separation or divorce.

The way that parents ultimately decide to divide time and parenting responsibilities is far less important than it is for each parent to maintain a calm and supportive home environment where children feel physically safe and emotionally secure.

No one expects you to be superhuman and avoid all parenting arguments. Indeed, sometimes intense arguing is the only way to reach a consensus. Nevertheless, one of the best things you can do for your children during this stressful period in their lives is to keep any such arguments out of their earshot. Children experience an attack on a parent as an attack on a part of themselves, so it is particularly difficult for them to hear one parent denigrate or "put down" the other. They need to feel free to love both parents, and to know that they can rely on both parents for support, without being pushed in any way to make choices between them. A choice about where a child will live must never be framed as a choice about who will or will not continue to act as a parent.

Unfortunately, conflict between parents cannot always be easily managed. Circumstances surrounding the breakdown of a relationship often lead to one or both former partners harboring raw and painful feelings. If such feelings make it impossible—temporarily at least—to maintain civility, the next best approach may be for you to reduce contact with each other. A therapist, parenting counselor, or parenting coach can help with practical aspects that require contact, such as transferring children between homes. Sometimes a good option is to arrange, at least short-term, for transfers to take place in a neutral location, or through an intermediary, such as a relative or a babysitter. You can limit communication, whenever possible, to texting and emailing. Give copies of your parenting plan to anyone who cares for your children, such as teachers and day-care providers, so that they are clear on who is allowed to pick children up and when. Make sure older children have clear instructions about where they are to be at all times, and who is and isn't allowed to pick them up.

Parents often find that high emotions diminish with the passage of time, allowing collaboration to gradually improve. Sometimes, however, one or both parents remain stuck in negative patterns of interaction. This can be enormously frustrating, particularly if you feel that you are the sane parent, and that you are constantly being driven to distraction by the unreasonable antics of the other parent. If you find yourself in this unfortunate position, get help for yourself. Therapy can help you protect your own emotions, and you will be a better parent when you are emotionally healthy.

One of your biggest challenges may be learning to refrain from interjecting yourself into minor disagreements between your child and the other parent. If the other parent is not emotionally capable of collaboration, trying to intervene is likely to be pointless at best and at worst, it may result in making the situation worse. The best way to protect yourself from emotional manipulation is to maintain an arms-length style of interaction indefinitely. You will need to teach your children to resolve disagreements with their other parent directly. Make an exception, of course, if a disagreement involves a major life decision or a serious safety issue, but barring that, step out of the way. Your children will learn to adapt to different rules and expectations at each parent's home, and to stand up for themselves when necessary.

If you are committed to a parenting arrangement that includes joint legal custody and relatively equal parenting time with children, it is essential that you find a way to reduce conflict and learn to communicate in a collaborative manner. If this is ultimately not possible, you may have more success with a plan that clearly divides responsibility for major decisions and requires children to move back and forth between homes less frequently.

Providing Support for Children

It is especially important in contentious custody battles to ensure that children receive emotional support. Almost all children who are going through or have gone through their parents' separation or divorce will benefit from some kind of counseling or family therapy. Sometimes children blame themselves, or harbor anger against one or both parents. With divorce being so commonplace today, there is no reason for any child to feel alone with these kinds of feelings. Participating in therapy or special support groups for children can help them heal emotionally.

If you have joint custody and your child's other parent does not agree that you should be providing this kind of emotional support for your children, speak to a family law attorney about how to handle this. You may need to obtain a court order.

When Children Refuse to Comply with Parenting Plans

Children resist following parenting plans for all kinds of reasons. They may be uncomfortable at one parent's home because of the relationship with that parent, or they may be uncomfortable for a completely unrelated reason. For example, all of their sources of comfort and entertainment may be located at the other parent's home. If your child constantly resists spending time with you, try to find out all of the reasons. Simply giving in to a child's refusal to comply with a parenting time agreement can result in the situation becoming an entrenched pattern. This is not generally in the best interests of the children, who need to know that both parents are committed to fulfilling parental roles. Nevertheless, forcing children to comply with a plan can backfire, potentially increasing resistance.

If you are the affected parent and you are on good terms with the other parent, the two of you can discuss potential solutions, such as adjusting the schedule or duplicating certain items at both homes. Be sure to listen carefully to any concerns your children may have as well. Even young children tend to be more compliant with parental decisions when they feel involved and heard. Beginning around age twelve, children need increasing input into the decision-making process to ensure that their age-appropriate needs for independence are being met. If you are unable to resolve a situation after conferring with the other parent and allowing children any appropriate input, you can request mediation to try to work it out. If the other parent refuses to attend mediation, or if mediation alone does not lead to a solution, and you are being shut-out of your child's life, the best next step may be to ask the court to appoint a parenting coordinator, and/or to order reunification therapy. Both of these options are discussed in detail below, under "Court-Appointed Services and Experts."

Addressing Potential "Parental Alienation Syndrome"

Parental alienation syndrome (PAS) is a campaign of alienation (either intentional or accidental) carried out by one parent against the other, resulting in the child developing strong feelings against the targeted parent.

Mental health experts have recently recognized that parental alienation can be a significant factor in child custody case. Experts recognize three levels of parental alienators:

- **Naïve alienators** - parents who recognize the value to a child of a healthy relationship with each parent but still occasionally denigrate the other parent in the child's presence;
- **Active alienators** - parents who regularly make denigrating remarks about the other parent in a child's presence; and
- **Obsessed alienators** - parents who are intentionally attempting to destroy a child's relationship with the other parent.

Family law judges are very aware of the potential damage to a child's emotional health that exists when one parent expresses hostile feelings toward the other parent in the child's presence. Nevertheless, not all judges recognize PAS as a valid syndrome, and those who do tend to focus on the more severe instances of behavior. A certain degree of "naïve alienation" in separating partners is quite common, as high emotions can make self-control difficult for even the most conscientious parents. If you believe your child's other parent may be making occasional negative comments to your child about you, the best first course of action is probably to broach it directly, pointing out that it isn't good for children to hear those things. If the other parent does not acknowledge your concerns as valid, you can suggest that they consult a family therapist about the issue, rather than taking your word for anything.

If your situation has gone beyond this, and you are certain that repeated negative comments by the other parent are affecting your relationship with your child, you have a right to raise this in court. It could be a basis for limiting the other parent's time with the children, as well as for implementation of other remedies, such a court-ordered family counseling for you and your children. You may need to hire a child custody evaluator to make your case. It can be challenging to produce convincing evidence that parental alienation is the source of a child's negative feelings toward one parent. Negative feelings might be due primarily to a campaign by the other parent, or they might be due primarily to something else, such as general family upheaval or the child's direct interactions with the non-favored parent. There are grounds for concern, however, if a child shows unmitigated hostility or resentment towards one parent with no objective basis for such feelings. If you believe that PAS is a significant factor in your custody case, discuss this with a child custody attorney who can help you explore your options.

Case Studies: Working to Reach an Out-of-Court Agreement

Jim and Cassie had once been crazy about each other, but they had always had some trouble getting along. Jim was an outgoing daredevil, while Cassie was a quiet homebody. Jim was a bit of a neat freak, while Cassie didn't mind a mess. There was nothing Jim loved more than a good rack of ribs on the barbecue. Cassie, of course, was a strict vegetarian. The list went on and on. When they were dating their differences had seemed manageable and even amusing. After four years of marriage and a child though, they were mutually annoying, even infuriating.

After Cassie filed for divorce, the court sent the couple to parenting mediation to see if they could reach an agreement on custody of two-year-old Melissa, but it did not go well. Cassie wanted sole custody, and the most she was willing to offer Jim was one overnight every other Saturday, and one midweek afternoon visit on the alternate weeks. "I've stayed home with Melissa since her birth," she argued, "while you have never been around. You have no idea how to take care of a toddler!"

When Jim protested that he loved Melissa and wanted to be a good father, Cassie just dug in her heels. "I don't believe you," she said. "I think you just want to spend more time with her so that you don't have to pay me as much child support."

<u>Attorney Consultation</u>

Jim shared his frustration with attorney Lily Needham. "Cassie seems to have gone crazy," he complained. "I'm not even asking for equal parenting time. I work long hours in investment banking, so I don't think I could manage that right now. But shouldn't I at least be able to have Melissa for two full weekends a month and one overnight during the week?"

"She is being a bit unreasonable," Ms. Needham agreed. "What we need to figure out though, is why. I know her attorney and he's a very rational guy. Let me talk to him and see if Cassie will agree to go to private mediation. If so, you and I can meet again first. I'm a pretty good coach, and if necessary, I can refer you to a therapist who can help you as well."

"I don't need a therapist!" Jim protested. "She's the one who's nuts!"

"The therapist isn't because I think you're nuts, Jim. It's because I think maybe you could use some help learning how to talk to Cassie. For example, I don't recommend calling her crazy."

That made Jim stop and think a bit. Maybe the attorney had a point. He had been pretty critical of Cassie.

Mediation Preparation and Divorce Coaching

To Jim's relief, Cassie agreed to go to private mediation. Jim met with Ms. Needham briefly to prepare for the first session. She gave him some child support calculations to share with Cassie. These would help him show her how little difference there would be in the amount he paid if Melissa spent the additional time with him that he was requesting, and would also show that he would be using that difference to pay for Melissa's meals and other incidentals while she was with him.

After they talked a bit more, Ms. Needham referred him to Dr. Sharp, a family therapist with a lot of experience in divorce coaching. Jim spent about an hour with Dr. Sharp, discussing his history and current dynamic with Cassie.

"We know that Cassie is worried about money and financial security," Dr. Sharp observed, but it seems to me that there is something deeper going on for her. It's pretty clear that she has a lot of anxiety."

"She does have a lot of anxiety," Jim agreed. "She's ridiculous about it. Everything scares her."

"Well," Dr. Sharp answered. "It might be true that she is overanxious. But it's also possible that since you are a self-professed 'big risk taker,' she has some reason to feel that you might not be sufficiently attentive to Melissa."

Jim thought this over. He had often made fun of Cassie for being so nervous about everything. He had only meant it as teasing, but he realized now that she probably had not found it funny. "I would never put Melissa in danger," he told Dr. Sharp. "What can I do to make Cassie understand that?"

Dr. Sharp urged Jim to immediately take some small steps that might be meaningful to Cassie. For example, he could get his apartment professionally child-proofed and sign up for a child-care class that included CPR training. He could then start off the mediation telling Cassie he had done these things, while explaining to her how much he cared about Melissa and how aware he was of the amount of attention a toddler needed.

"Another thing you could try," Dr. Sharp went on, "is to agree to start out with the schedule that Cassie had already agreed to, but ask her to include a daily Skype call of 15 minutes or so every evening so that Melissa will be able to see your face and hear your voice on a regular basis. Then propose something like the following: after the first month, you change one of the Saturday nights to a full weekend; after another month or two, build in the second full weekend; and then eventually, move the mid-week dinner to an overnight as well. You can also assure

Cassie that you will call her before leaving Melissa with a babysitter."

"Be open to negotiation on the timing," Dr. Sharp suggested. "You can stretch things out for a few more months if that makes Cassie more comfortable, but don't stretch it out for too long, because at Melissa's age she needs to keep seeing you on a regular basis to maintain bonding. Be sure to build the changes in as firm dates in your written agreement. Otherwise, she might backtrack."

Progress in Mediation

Jim followed Dr. Sharp's advice, and he was pleasantly surprised at how quickly they made progress in mediation. Melissa didn't agree to everything after the first session, but she was clearly moving closer. Jim met with both Dr. Sharp and Ms. Needham again before the second session, during which they planned to discuss financial matters. As Dr. Sharp had suspected, Melissa's anxiety flared up at the mere mention of money, and she again began to make extreme demands. Thanks to his preparation, however, instead of reacting with anger, Jim was able to keep his cool and come up with some ideas that made Cassie feel less apprehensive. After a few more sessions, they resolved all of their issues and were able to file a settlement agreement with the court.

Chapter 4

Child Custody Decisions in New Jersey Courts

A few parents will not be able to agree on a parenting plan even after extensive negotiation and mediation and will eventually find themselves in court. This is especially common when one parent has serious concerns about the other. Sometimes discussions are ineffective because one parent has an issue with addiction or abusive behavior. If you are having trouble agreeing on a parenting plan, for whatever reason, the following information may help give you get a better idea of what kind of custody decision a judge might make in your case.

If you still have questions after reading this, a consultation with a family law attorney may be in order.

The New Jersey Child Custody Statute

Courts in New Jersey making child custody decisions are bound to follow the New Jersey custody statute, N.J.S.A. 9:2-4. This statute, along with others applicable to children and parents, is included in Title 9 of the New Jersey Statutes Annotated (N.J.S.A.), available on-line from the New Jersey Legislature. Several other chapters in Title 9 also affect decisions and agreements regarding child custody.

The New Jersey custody statute declares that the public policy of the state is to assure minor children of separated or divorced parents "frequent and continuing contact with both parents." It further states that parental sharing of "the rights and responsibilities of child rearing" is "in the public interest." (N.J.S.A. 9:2-4). These basic premises do not mean that the law favors any particular form of child custody. There are many potential parenting plans that will satisfy the law.

Factors under the Statute

As we have already discussed, the statute is gender-neutral. New Jersey law does not favor the interests of either parent over the other; rather, it elevates a child's best interests above all else. While the starting assumption is that frequent and continuing contact with two parents who are sharing parental rights and responsibilities is in a child's best interests, there are many additional factors that courts making custody decisions must consider. The factors listed in the child support statute are as follows:

58

- the parents' ability to agree, communicate and cooperate in matters relating to the child,
- the parents' willingness to accept custody and any history of unwillingness to allow parenting time not based on substantiated abuse,
- the interaction and relationship of the child with parents and siblings,
- any history of domestic violence,
- the safety of the child and either parent from physical abuse by the other parent,
- the preference of a child who is of sufficient age and capacity to reason so as to form an intelligent decision,
- the child's needs,
- the stability of the home environment offered,
- the quality and continuity of the child's education,
- the parent's fitness,
- the geographical proximity of the parents' homes,
- the extent and quality of the time spent with the child prior to or subsequent to the separation,
- each parents' employment responsibilities, and
- the ages and number of children.

(N.J.S.A. 9:2-4.)

Courts are also free to consider any additional factors that could impact the child's best interests. Closer examination of some of the above factors can be helpful in understanding exactly what courts look for when making custody decisions:

- **Children's Physical Health and Safety**. A judge may limit either parent's contact with a child to supervised visitation if either parent appears to pose a substantial risk of harm to the child. This could be due to a history of domestic violence, or to some other circumstance. In an extreme case, a judge may even disallow visitation entirely. In most situations, however, a court will find that it is in the child's best interests to have some contact with each parent. Restrictions on visitation are generally subject to modification if a parent can demonstrate that the conditions necessitating the restriction no longer exist. If you are a parent whose time with a child has been restricted due to safety concerns, it is in your own best interests, as well as the best interests of your child, to comply strictly with all court requirements.

- **Children's Developmental, Social and Emotional Needs**. Although New Jersey law does not favor either mothers or fathers based on gender, courts do consider children's age-related developmental needs. In assessing such needs, judges consider the general stability of the environment in each parent's home, as well as the quality of the interaction between the child and each parent. The extent to which each parent has participated in child care prior to the court's decision is an important consideration, as this establishes both the parent's ongoing commitment to assuming parental responsibilities and the probable strength of the parent-child bond. Courts also consider sibling relationships to be very important and will usually try very hard to keep siblings together.

If you are a father with a long history of full involvement in parenting, you will probably be easily able to demonstrate your commitment to your child's social, emotional, and developmental needs. If, on the other hand, you have taken a secondary role up to this point, do not assume that this automatically means that you cannot now become an equal participant. Many fathers, particularly those who were raised in more traditional households or who have been pursuing particularly demanding careers, do not have a history of full involvement in child care. If this is your history and you would like things to change, start by expressing your desire to be helpful. Try to step up to take on some of the less appealing tasks of parenting, and become involved in any way possible. All aspects of the relationship between a parent and child are important in assessing the child's needs, including the parent's regular engagement in extracurricular activities and regular interaction with other adults who care for the child, such as babysitters, day care providers, teachers, counselors, and coaches. Now is the time to reassess your activities and your priorities to put the best face forward on your parenting case. You can find more tips on presenting your case in "Preparing for Court," later in this book.

- **A Child's Own Preferences**. The law allows children who have attained sufficient intellectual and emotional maturity to be able to provide intelligent input into the custody decision to state a preference. The statute does not specify an exact age, and a judge will evaluate each child's maturity individually. Generally speaking, however, children who are close to 12 years of age, or older, will be allowed input. A child's preference is only one factor, and like all factors, it will be given more or less weight depending on all other circumstances. If a child does not spontaneously reveal a preference, parents would be wise to avoid directly asking the child's opinion. Children often experience feelings of betrayal toward one parent when pressed to make a choice. A parent should under no circumstances ever make a child feel guilty for having expressed a preference.

Sometimes either the judge or a guardian ad litem (GAL) will interview the child, but they will do so out of the courtroom in a way that carefully avoids forcing the child to make direct statements about preferences. You can find more information about GAL's below, under "Court-Appointed Services and Experts."

- **Co-Parenting and Communication Skills**. Parents who wish to share both legal and physical custody need to demonstrate superior co-parenting abilities, since such arrangements require parents to collaborate closely with one other. While each parent's willingness to be actively involved in a child's life is important, parents must also be careful not to interfere with the child's relationship with the other parent. If either parent demonstrates an unfounded desire or intention to prevent a child from having significant contact with the other parent, the interfering parent will find themselves at a disadvantage.

- **Parental Fitness**. Parents will not be found "unfit" unless their conduct has a substantial adverse effect on the child. It is generally unwise to raise every conceivably negative aspect of the other parent's personality in court. If there is an aspect of the latter's conduct that poses a threat to a child, it is, of course, critical to highlight this. Raising minor and everyday issues however, can backfire by making the complaining parent appear petty and vindictive.

- **Practical Considerations.** In spite of everyone's sincere wishes and best intentions, practical considerations can sometimes be the difference between one kind of custody order and another. The distance between the parents' homes, the location of a child's school, parents' respective employment responsibilities, and the number and ages of any other children in each home, can all impact what kind of arrangement will really work for a family. Courts do their best to look at all of the circumstances in each case.

  If you are concerned about practical factors, you can try to make adjustments if this is within their power. For example, if you are a father who has spent 80 hours a week at work for the past few years, you may truly be ready to scale back work responsibilities in order to spend more time with your children. If you have a choice of living arrangements, you can prioritize a choice that is closer to a child's school or to the child's other home. These can be extremely difficult decisions to make. Fathers who deeply desire to spend more time with children, but also want to continue working hard to maintain a standard of living for those children, can find themselves caught in a dilemma. If this applies to you, be sure to communicate your desire to do whatever is in your children's best interests to everyone involved in the decision-making process, especially the other parent.

Child Custody Hearings and Trials

If you are successful in working out a parenting agreement with your child's other parent, you may never need to appear in court. You will, however, need to file your agreement in the Family Part of the New Jersey Superior Court to ensure that it is finalized into an enforceable court order. If you are not able to work things out, then you may end up in a hearing or trial. This book does not go into detail regarding the paperwork required to complete a New Jersey divorce or a stand-alone child custody case. You can find information on filing requirements on the Weinberger Divorce & Family Law Group website, as well as in our other e-books on Contested Divorce and Uncontested Divorce. You can also find information at the New Jersey Courts Self-Help Resource Center.

In general, after one parent has commenced a court case, there will be several procedures that precede a final hearing or trial. The exact sequence will depend on various circumstances, including whether the complaint is part of a divorce or is a separate custody case, which county the complaint is filed in, and which judge is hearing the case. In all situations, New Jersey courts give custody and visitation issues high priority and will attempt to resolve them as quickly as possible.

- **Parenting Classes**. New Jersey requires most parents with legal issues regarding custody, parenting time, or child support to attend parenting education programs. Typically, a family law mediator and two social workers will present information about how parental separation and family conflict tends to impact children and how parents can make things easier for children and limit potential negative effects. Each parent attends the class separately. If you are scheduled to attend a class, be sure to take this seriously. Failure to attend could impact the courts parenting decisions.

- **Court-Mandated Mediation**. Unless there is an unusual situation that applies to your family, such as a restraining order for domestic violence, New Jersey courts will also require you to participate in free and confidential parenting mediation to try to resolve your disagreements early in a divorce or custody case. Parents attend these mediation sessions without attorneys. A court-appointed mediator will help you try to come to an agreement on custody and parenting. If you do reach an agreement it will be formalized and made binding after the mediation.

Preparing for Court

Early Decision-Making

An important decision you may need to make early in your case is whether or not to move out of the family home. Fathers who wish to seek primary or shared residential custody should be aware that leaving the home may be construed by the court as some indication of a voluntary relinquishment of the primary parenting role. In addition, keeping children in the family home could be viewed as part of maintaining consistency for them, which would put the parent still living there at somewhat of an advantage. If you are considering leaving the family home, it is a good idea to consult a family law attorney first. There are some situations where this will be the best decisions, but exercise caution first.

Keeping Good Records

Early in a separation, even if you seem to be working things out well with the other parent, it is a good idea to document exactly what each of you is doing and to track the time each of you is spending with your child. This is even more critical if things get off on a more contentious footing. If you share legal custody with your child's other parent, or you do not yet have orders regarding legal custody, keep the other parent informed of all important events, any necessary changes to the parenting schedule, and any medical, extracurricular, or similar issues affecting your child. Programs like "Family Wizard" can ease the chore of maintaining a joint family calendar. If you do end up having to go to court at any point, a daily diary noting conversations and events in real time can provide back-up for your testimony. If the other parent has chronic issues complying with the schedule, note these issues in writing as they occur.

If you want more time with your children and believe that the other parent is blocking this, document any conversations that back up your position. Make and document specific offers to help with things that you believe would be beneficial for your children. In short, keep records of all but the most insignificant communications that you have with the other parent. If parenting responsibilities have recently changed, and you believe that past patterns are more indicative of the long-term division of duties, create a retroactive calendar demonstrating the previous state of affairs. This is particularly important if you believe that the other parent is putting on a temporary show of great involvement for the court. A longstanding history of noninvolvement may cause the court to question whether the new level is likely to be sustainable over time.

All of this documentation can help you make your arguments in court, whether you are attempting to establish custody, or whether you need to request a legal remedy for violation of custody orders, such as a change in parenting time or compensatory time. There is more information on enforcing custody orders and seeking remedies for violations of such orders later in this book.

While it might seem like nitpicking to detail time spent on specific activities—or time that you would like to spend on specific activities, if you believe that you are being blocked—this can be a very persuasive tool in an argument for more time. Try to describe your contributions both in hours per week and in percentages of time per parent. The applicable activities a court might consider will vary depending on a child's age, but the following are some broad examples:

- Feeding,
- Shopping for groceries and preparing meals,
- Helping with bathing, teeth brushing, or other hygiene related tasks,
- Doing laundry,
- Shopping for clothing,
- Cleaning house,
- Assigning and assisting with chores,

- Helping with pet care,
- Playing games or doing crafts,
- Taking vacation trips,
- Planning vacations,
- Planning parties
- Choosing birthday or holiday gifts,
- Helping to buy gifts for child's friends,
- Making regular time for conversation,
- Teaching a child reading, cooking, or other skills,
- Setting limits and enforcing household rules,
- Helping with homework,
- Participating in bedtime rituals, such as story-reading,
- Driving to various appointments and activities,
- Accompanying child on appointments such as doctor and dentist visits,
- Attending the child's sporting events, recitals, parent-teacher conferences or other important events,
- Taking off work to stay home with a sick child.

If applicable, in addition to specifying all the ways that you have participated as a parent, you may want to point out the percentage of time the other parent has been out of town or otherwise unavailable due to work or other commitments.

Presenting Evidence About the Other Parent

If you find yourself in a court battle, refrain from attacking the other parent on any lifestyle or behavior choice that does not impact their ability to be a good parent. This applies both to any written information you provide to the court, and to any testimony you may eventually give during a deposition or a court hearing. If you are going through a divorce that includes a custody battle, you may be tempted to bring up every way that your spouse behaved improperly during your marriage. The court, however, will not care if your spouse cheated, lied, or just generally behaved badly, unless such behavior negatively impacted the children or rose to the level of domestic abuse. Family law judges are acutely aware that it is possible for a person to be a poor romantic or marital partner, but still be a good parent. Similarly, if your former partner has a new love interest, a court will not care whether or not that person is spending time in your former partner's home, unless there is something about this new love interest that clearly puts the children at risk. Focus your criticisms on parenting abilities only. If your former partner did not take on an equal share of parenting responsibilities, point this out. If she did something that put the children at risk, by all means, point that out as well.

Court-Appointed Services and Experts

If your case proceeds to court, it is very likely that you will interact with one or more court-appointed professionals. The cost of hiring such professionals often falls on the parents, particularly on the parent with greater financial means. The more contentious your case, the more professionals you are likely to encounter, and the more expensive and protracted your case is likely to become. The involvement of professionals may have a positive effect on the outcome of your case. On the other hand, limiting litigation as much as possible may preserve funds that could be used to care for children and provide them with a comfortable home, a good education and enriching extracurricular activities. Whether or not to proceed further with a custody or visitation claim is often a difficult judgment call in the face of mounting costs. Understanding how court-approved professionals may or may not contribute to a desired result can be a crucial factor in the decision. The following information may be helpful:

Custody Evaluators:

Child Custody Evaluators are licensed mental health experts, such as psychiatrists, psychologists, social workers and professional counselors. They have additional training in the law governing child custody and parenting. The most qualified evaluators also have extensive experience working with high-conflict families in separation and divorce. Depending on the circumstances, an evaluator can be court appointed or hired by one or both parents.

Custody evaluators work for an hourly fee and generally require a retainer before beginning to perform services. Parents are generally responsible for paying the fees, and can therefore save a considerable amount of money by agreeing to hire one joint evaluator. It is common, however for each parent to retain an individual expert. A court may also appoint its own custody expert. The opinion of an expert retained by the court is not given any greater weight than the opinion of an expert retained by the parents. Evaluators are required to consider the best interests of the child, regardless of who is paying their bills. They conduct in-depth evaluations of each parent through personal interviews and psychological testing. They also meet with children, usually both individually and together with each parent. Some evaluators make home visits to observe children in a more natural setting. If necessary, they may interview others involved with the children such as teachers or other caregivers. The evaluator prepares a report for the court and may testify as an expert witness.

Family law judges give great weight to the recommendations of child custody evaluators. When there is only one evaluator, a judge is very likely to follow the evaluator's recommendations to at least a substantial degree. If there is more than one, the judge can decide which is more credible. If there is an extreme difference in findings and recommendations, the case may proceed to trial. During the trial, the evaluators will testify as to their findings and conclusions, and will be subject to cross-examination.

Parents meeting with custody evaluators are often nervous. For the most part, the best advice is to present a clean and neat appearance, be honest, and act naturally with your children. Answer all questions as completely and directly as possible. Avoid speaking badly of the other parent unless you must raise an issue in response to direct questions. In general, evaluators are looking for your ability to understand your children's needs, set appropriate boundaries, and provide them with a proper environment. They will assess the strength of the bond between you and your children by observing your interaction. It is a good idea to meet with your attorney to prepare before you meet with an evaluator.

Guardians ad Litem (GALs):

A "guardian ad litem," or GAL, acts on behalf of another person during a particular law suit. "Ad litem" means "for the suit." New Jersey courts occasionally appoint GALs in high conflict child custody cases when there is a risk of a child's best interests becoming lost in the battle between the parents. One of the parents may request the appointment, or the judge may make it independently. New Jersey GALs may be mental health professionals, attorneys, or laypersons. They must possess education and experience in child custody law and child development, particularly in the context of high conflict divorcing families. The GAL does not directly represent a child, but instead acts as an independent fact finder, investigator, and evaluator to determine what will further the child's best interests. A GAL might ask a judge who has not already done so to appoint other professionals to protect the child's interests and assist the GAL, such as a child custody evaluator or a parenting coordinator. Parents generally pay for the GAL's services.

A GAL completes an investigation and then provides the court with a neutral and objective opinion and a report regarding what kind of parenting arrangements would be in the best interests of the children. A GAL generally interviews the children, the parents, and any other people with information relevant to the case, such as caregivers, teachers, counselors, and family members. The GAL will also review documentary evidence, including reports and recommendations from professionals familiar with the child, such as social workers, child psychologists, doctors, and teachers. The parents and the attorneys in the case can also provide the GAL with information and opinions. The GAL may testify in court and the parents can present evidence that either supplements or contracts the opinion of the GAL.

Parenting Coordinators:

Parenting coordinators are usually licensed mental health professionals, attorneys, or qualified lay persons. They are trained in family mediation and should be familiar with child development, high conflict families, and the negative impacts of long-term custody disputes on

72

children. They are neutral toward the parents and committed to supporting the best interests of the child. A parent can ask the court to appoint a parenting coordinator or the court can make the appointment on its own. In some cases, a PC will be appointed in conjunction with a Guardian ad Litem (GAL) or a custody evaluator. A GAL or a custody evaluator will also sometimes recommend that the court appoint a Parenting Coordinator. If there is no court order for the appointment, the parents must sign a stipulation.

Parenting coordination, like mediation, is a form of alternative dispute resolution. Unlike mediation, however, it is not confidential. The coordinator interacts directly with the family and monitors parental behaviors, and can thus provide additional information to assist a GAL or a custody evaluator. The coordinator may serve for a predetermined time or may have an open-ended appointment. In the latter case, parents who make initial progress but have trouble maintaining a good co-parenting relationship can return to the coordinator when new conflicts arise.

Parenting coordinators are expected to appear in court if necessary, but unlike child custody evaluators or guardians ad litem, they make recommendations to parents or their attorneys rather than directly to the court. Their first priority is to bring the parents into agreement for the benefit of the child. Goals of parenting coordination include shielding children from family conflict and related stress and helping them feel free to love both parents. The coordinator works directly with the parents to improve their abilities to communicate effectively, manage anger, and collaborate on a clear parenting plan. They also monitor parental behaviors and compliance with court orders with the ultimate goal of reducing contentious court filings and litigation.

Parenting coordinators generally collaborate with all other professionals involved with the family. If necessary, the coordinator may refer family members for services such as individual or family counseling, drug screenings, parenting classes, or reconciliation therapy. Because judges are not generally permitted to delegate their enforcement authority, the power of a parenting coordinator is limited. If an order or agreements permits, the coordinator can recommend temporary changes in the parenting schedule or to terms such as pick-up and drop-off arrangements. However, a court cannot simply order parents to comply with a parenting coordinator's recommendations without judicial review.

Parenting coordination is much more successful when both parents support the process and the process is implemented early in a case. A New Jersey pilot program in parenting coordination was discontinued in 2012, largely because the program was unable to intervene early enough to prevent conflict-ridden patterns of interaction from becoming entrenched. The court will still order appointment of a parenting coordinator in an appropriate case.

It is important to distinguish parenting coordination from "co-parenting counseling" or "parent coaching." Parenting coordination is not confidential, and a parenting coordinator may be required to share information with the court. Co-parent counseling is a type of family therapy or family counseling. Like a parenting coordinator, a co-parenting counselor addresses issues associated with family reorganizations, but the services of a coordinator are more structured and more directive. Coordinators work primarily with parents who are experiencing serious conflict, or whose own emotional issues are interfering with their parenting abilities. Parents with lower levels of conflict may benefit from co-parenting counseling and can take advantage of such services without court intervention.

Reunification Therapists:

Reunification therapy is a type of family counseling designed to help "reunify" children with a marginalized parent. Regardless of whether your relationship with your child has been damaged by a campaign of alienation carried out by the other parent, or by the high conflict and general family disruption of divorce, reunification therapy may help you repair the relationship. You can ask a court to order reunification therapy if one or more of your children stops following your agreed-upon or court-ordered parenting plan. The court will appoint a qualified therapist who has knowledge and experience working with family disruption in divorce.

A court order for reunification therapy requires both parents to cooperate. The order should outline specific concerns and treatment goals, define appropriate interventions, set parameters for involvement of extended family members, specify payment arrangements, and outline consequences for non-compliance with the order. If complicating issues exist, such as a history of alcohol or substance abuse, mental illness, incarceration, or any kind of past domestic violence, the order must also set up parameters to ensure that all contact between family members will be safe. The reunification therapist will have access to any prior pertinent records from other professionals or agencies.

A reunification therapist works with the entire family for the best interests of the child or children in question. In general, the goal will be to increase the amount of time a child spends with the non-favored parent. Neither parent directs the therapy and information shared with the therapist is not confidential. The therapist must report significant findings and positive or negative outcomes back to the court. The therapist will meet separately with each family member and will review any custody evaluations and current court orders or parenting agreements related to custody or visitation. The therapist may also consult with other involved professionals, such as a parenting coordinator.

If the custodial parent is not supportive of reunification therapy, the therapist will provide education that focuses on how the goals of the therapy are in the best interests of the children. A successful therapist does not assign blame or force quick resolutions, but rather builds trust and enlists both parent in working toward positive results for children. Therapy addresses ongoing issues and gradually builds in outside visits between the child and the affected parent, usually starting with brief, fun activities.

At least eight to twelve sessions with increasingly frequent outside visits is generally recommended, during which time the therapist will keep the court apprised of progress. Therapy results vary, not only according to the history of each parent-child relationship, but also according to the ongoing interaction of all personalities in the family. The therapist will also submit a final report to the court at the conclusion of the process. A family law attorney can provide more information on reunification therapy.

Law Guardians:

Law guardians are sometimes confused with guardians ad litem, but their roles are quite different. Law Guardians are licensed attorneys who act as independent legal advocates for the best interests of children and take an active part in hearings. New Jersey courts are required to appoint law guardians for children when they are the subjects of litigation against their parents or guardians concerning alleged abuse, neglect or possible termination of parental rights. (N.J.S.A. §§ 9:6-8.23 and 30:4C-15.4(b)). The New Jersey Office of the Public Defender maintains an Office of Law Guardian that provides representation for children in such cases. A law guardian may represent more than one child in a family.

Law guardians gather relevant information and may visit children at home or at school to talk to them about their case and help them understand what will happen in court. They may also coordinate expert evaluations of the child, such as mental health evaluations. A law guardian works to understand both the child's preferences and the child's overall best interests and will communicate these to the court.

A law guardian does not represent either parent. If a court has appointed a law guardian to represent your child, you may want to consult with an experienced New Jersey family law attorney to ensure protection of your own interests and legal rights.

Attorneys for Children in Custody Cases:

In addition to appointing law guardians in child neglect and abuse cases, judges can appoint attorneys for children in cases where custody, visitation or parenting time is an issue, either on application of a party or on the court's own motion. This is not a common occurrence, but it may be appropriate when a trial court determines that the child's best interests are not being sufficiently protected by the attorneys for the parents in the case. Parents are generally required to pay for the fees and costs of the child's attorney. The role of the court-appointed attorney for a child is often confused with the role of a GAL. The differences between these two roles is further explained in New Jersey Court Rule 5:8B. An experienced child custody attorney can provide more information on attorneys for children in child custody cases.

Custody and Visitation Orders When Parents and Children Live in Different States

If you are a New Jersey father whose child lives in a different state, or if your child lives in New Jersey but you do not, you may have questions about which court has authority to create orders controlling child custody and visitation. Parents often object to orders coming from a court to which they lack easy access, or from a state whose laws are not favorable to them. While the issue of state authority or "jurisdiction" over parenting matters is complex, there are a few basic principles that generally guide the process. Only one state at a time can have jurisdiction over custody and visitation and can issue binding orders. Other states will enforce these orders but will not make changes unless a party successfully challenges the original court's authority, and the new state then accepts jurisdiction. This often happens when a child or both parents move out of the state.

Jurisdiction under the UCCJEA (N.J.S.A. 2A:34-53 et seq.)

Jurisdiction is usually simple when a child and both parents live in the same state. In other cases, it may be complicated and require assistance from a family law attorney. In general, jurisdiction must be based on one of the following circumstances:

- **Home State.** The most important question is which state is the child's "home state." A state is the home state if a child has resided there continuously for the six months preceding the custody action, or if the child resided there for six months prior to leaving the state and one of the parents—or a person acting as a parent—continues to live there. Once a child has lived in a new state for six consecutive months, that state ordinarily becomes the new home state.

- **Significant Connections.** Sometimes a child has moved around so much that there is no clear home state. In that case, a court will look at whether or not a child or the child's family has "significant connections" in the state and where most of the evidence relating to the custody claim is located. The court will consider questions such as where each parent is employed, where the child has spent the most time, where a child is currently enrolled in school, where a child's pediatrician is located, or where members of the child's extended family live.

- **Convenient Forum.** If there is no clear home state and a child has fairly equal and significant connections with more than one state, the court will consider which state creates a more convenient forum for the case. When there is an apparent tie between states, one court must eventually concede to avoid a situation of conflicting orders.

- **Emergency.** A court can accept emergency jurisdiction, often on a temporary basis, when a child who is in the state has been abandoned or needs protection from risk of abuse. This sometimes occurs when a parent flees a home state with a child to escape domestic violence.

- **Default.** The child's current state of residence will assume jurisdiction by default if there is no other state that has a better connection with the parties or the claims.

International Custody Disputes

If your child's other parent lives in another country or is planning to move to another country, the increased distance and potential interplay with the other country's laws can present serious challenges in trying to work out parental agreements.

The UCCJEA addresses the jurisdiction of foreign countries as well as states. It generally provides that states will treat custody orders entered in other countries as equal to those entered in the United States, if the country had proper jurisdiction to begin with and the custody order does not violate any fundamental human rights. New Jersey's version of the UCCJEA requires foreign courts to give all parties notice and an opportunity to be heard before making a custody determination, and also requires that custody decisions be based on the best interests of children.

A particularly difficult and traumatic situation can arise if one parent leaves the United States with a child without the consent of the other parent. The latter then has the right to ask the home state to enter custody and visitation orders. Enforcing those orders in a foreign country, however, may be a challenge. Any parent confronted with such a difficult circumstance will need to consult with a family law attorney who has experience with international custody disputes and is familiar with the Hague Convention.

The Hague Convention on the Civil Aspects of International Child Abduction

The Hague Conference on Private International Law is a world organization dedicated to cross-border cooperation. In 1988, the United States ratified resolutions proposed by a 1980 Hague convention to address the wrongful removal of children from home countries. The resolutions created treaty relationships between the U.S and more than 65 other countries. Countries comply with the treaties to variable degrees. More information is available from The Hague's Child Abduction Section and the Bureau of Consular Affairs of the United States Department of State; and the National Center for Missing & Exploited Children. The Office of Children's Issues at the Bureau of Consular Affairs handles cases regarding children who are wrongfully removed either to or from the United States.

Parents who file Hague applications and receive a custody hearing in a foreign country may need to hire an attorney who can represent them in that country.

Requirements of The Hague Application:

A parent can file a Hague Application within one year following the wrongful removal from the home country - also called "the country of habitual residence" - of a child who was under the age of 16 at the time of removal. The parent does not have to have a custody order in effect but must have been exercising a right of custody (actually visiting with and caring for the child to some degree) at the time the child was removed or retained in the foreign country and must not have consented to the removal or retention.

A parent who removes a child often returns the child voluntarily when the other parent files a Hague Application.

A parent who instead chooses to oppose a child's return has the burden of proving that one of the following exceptions applies:

- There is a grave risk that the child's return would expose the child to physical or psychological harm or otherwise place the child in an intolerable situation,
- The child objects to being returned and is sufficiently mature for the court to take this into account, or
- The return would violate fundamental principles of human rights and freedoms according to the country where the child is being held.

It is not always possible to predict how different countries will interpret this law and reach a result. Mediation is sometimes a helpful option. You can speak to a State Department case officer at the Office of Children's Issues (toll free at 1 (888) 407-4747) to obtain more information.

Case Studies: How Courts Make Custody Decisions

The following example provides a detailed picture of how an initial disagreement might develop into a court battle, including several steps that a family would be likely to go through along the way. Although the couple is fictional, the analysis is adapted and summarized from actual court decisions under the New Jersey custody statute:

<u>Initial Parenting Arrangement</u>

During their five-year relationship, Miranda and Ryan lived in Woolwich Township, New Jersey, where Ryan worked as a real estate agent and Miranda worked as a technical writer. Both had flexible schedules, and after their daughter Desi was born, they shared parenting tasks fairly equally. Unfortunately, the relationship floundered, and when Desi was almost three, Miranda and Ryan decided to separate. Soon afterward, Miranda accepted a job in Piscataway, which provided her with increased income and greater job stability. To manage the commute, she moved into her parents' home in Bridgewater.

Miranda and Ryan decided not to go to court over custody and visitation. Instead, they worked out an unwritten parenting agreement between themselves. For over a year, they followed a 4-3-3-4 schedule. Desi spent Sundays through Tuesdays with Miranda and Thursdays through Saturdays with Ryan, while the parents alternated Wednesdays. They managed the nearly 90-mile drive between their homes by setting up a mid-way transfer point at a family restaurant. While the schedule worked fairly well, the amount of driving it necessitated was stressful for everyone. More concerning still was that Desi would soon start kindergarten, making the mid-week transfer no longer feasible.

The Conflict

Miranda insisted that she should start keeping Desi for full weeks, and that Ryan's time should be cut back to alternate weekends. Ryan protested, pointing out that he was an equal parent. "Why should you automatically get to be the main parent now?" he asked.

"She's a girl," Miranda answered, "of course she needs to be with her mother more than with her father."

Ryan wondered if Miranda was right. He considered just giving in, but the thought of losing so much time with Desi was too much. He consulted an attorney, Lindsey Moore, who told him that he had an equal right to be the primary parent, regardless of his gender. She asked Ryan if there were any other potential solutions, such as him moving closer to Miranda. Ryan didn't see this as feasible. All of his business contacts were in the south of the state, he explained, and he specialized in waterfront properties.

"Well then," Ms. Moore advised, "I can't guarantee you would win a case for primary custody, but we can try. At the very least, you should get more parenting time than Miranda is currently offering."

Both Parents File for Custody

After his consultation with Ms. Moore, Ryan told Miranda that he believed he had a right to equal time with Desi, but Miranda stayed firm. In spite of his continuing protests, she began to keep Desi with her for longer and longer periods of time. She also filed a custody case in family court, requesting to be named as primary residential parent. Ryan cross-complained with the same request.

The court then sent them to mandatory parenting mediation, but they failed to reach an agreement.

Eventually, each parent obtained separate child custody evaluations with recommended parenting schedules, and the court held a hearing to determine the best arrangement for Desi. Both of the custody experts analyzed the facts of the case in light of the factors set forth in N.J.S.A. 9:2-4(c). They offered their opinions, conclusions, and recommendations in written reports and in testimony. Miranda and Ryan also testified extensively at the hearing.

The Child Custody Evaluations and Reports

Miranda's expert, psychologist Martin Hagerty, interviewed both Ryan and Miranda multiple times at his office, both individually, and with Desi. Dr. Hagerty also made observational home visits. In addition, he interviewed Miranda's parents, who were acting as Desi's caretakers while Miranda was at work, as well as Ryan's sister, her husband, and their 14-year-old daughter, all of whom babysat regularly for Desi while Ryan worked.

Ryan's expert, psychologist Franklin Rosenstein, also conducted home visits and office interviews of Desi, and of each parent, both separately and with Desi. In addition, he evaluated each parent with multiple psychometric testing, including the MMPI-2, which focuses on personality and behavior. He also reviewed documentary materials provided by both parents, and telephonically interviewed the relatives/caregivers on both sides.

The experts agreed that the parents had historically seen themselves as equal parenting partners, and both experts commended the parents on their thoughtful and collaborative construction of a developmentally-appropriate and nurturing life for their daughter. Both experts also recommended that the parents continue to share parenting time as equally as possible. They agreed, however, that the current distance between homes was a major impediment to an exactly equal split.

Dr. Hagerty, Miranda's expert, recommended that Desi reside primarily with Miranda but spend three weekends per month and the majority of school vacations (including two weeks during the winter, one week during the spring and eight weeks during the summer) with Ryan. He further recommended that Miranda have four weekends during Ryan's eight summer weeks, and that the parents alternate time on specified major holidays. Dr. Hagerty added that whichever parent the child was not currently staying with should have one telephone, Skype, or FaceTime call per day, limited to about fifteen minutes. Dr. Hagerty's recommended schedule gave Miranda approximately 240 days per year to Ryan's 125 days per year.

Dr. Rosenstein, Ryan's expert, recommended a similar schedule, but with the primary parent flipped. During the school year Desi would reside with Ryan and spend only alternate weekends with Miranda. During the summers and major school breaks, the schedule would be reversed. Rosenstein noted the stress more frequent travel would impose on Desi. His recommended schedule gave Ryan approximately 260 days per year to Miranda's 105 days.

The Court's Observations and Findings of Fact

At the conclusion of the hearing, the court made findings of fact on each element of the child custody statute, noting first that since there was no evidence of domestic violence or safety concerns, and the child was an only child who was too young to state an intelligent preference, factors (4) through (6) and (14) of the statute were irrelevant. With respect to each of the remaining factors, the court made the following observations and findings:

(1)   The parents' ability to agree, communicate and cooperate in matters relating to the child:

The testimony and documentary evidence demonstrate that both parents initially communicated and cooperated on child-related matters at a high level. The father stated, however, that over the past year, the mother became hostile and denigrating toward his parental status, leading to a breakdown in communication and an inability to construct a reasonable new parenting plan. He testified that on several occasions, the mother had refused to transfer the child mid-week in accordance with their long-term agreement. The mother did not dispute this, but she justified her actions as an effort to help the child acclimate to an impending school schedule. The father stated that he went along with the mother's insistence only to protect the child from escalating conflict. He continued to comply with their agreed upon schedule as closely as possible.

Based on the uncontroverted testimony, the court finds that the father is more likely than the mother to communicate, seek discussion, and foster agreement on issues regarding the child.

(2)   The parents' willingness to accept custody and any history of unwillingness to allow parenting time not based on substantiated abuse:

Both parents have asserted their wish to act as primary custodians and the evidence shows that both have the capacity to do so. The mother has demonstrated some interference with the father's parenting time. The father has not done the same.

Based on the testimony and documentary evidence, the court finds that the father is more supportive of the child's relationship with the mother than she is of the child's relationship with him, and that the mother is more likely to interfere with the father's parenting time.

(3) The interaction and relationship of the child and the parents:

Based on the testimony and documentary evidence, the court finds that the child has a loving and positive relationship with both parents.

(7) The needs of the child:

Based on the testimony and documentary evidence, the court finds that both parents are attentive and devoted, and both have met the child's needs to date.

(8) The stability of the home environment offered:

Dr. Hagerty expressed no concerns in his report or testimony regarding the safety, general welfare, and well-being of the child in either parent's home. He noted Desi's close bond with her maternal grandparents and lauded the fact that her secondary caregivers were in the same home as her mother. Dr. Rosenstein essentially agreed with this. He also noted, however, that the mother had stated that she might eventually move out of her parents' home, while still professing a commitment to staying in the same neighborhood. Dr. Rosenstein also pointed out that the father had gone to extraordinary lengths to build his work schedule around parenting, that Desi had close ties to her paternal aunt and uncle and her cousins, and that of the two parents, the father appeared to be more available both before and after school hours.

Based on the testimony and documentary evidence, the court finds that both parents are equally able to provide the child with a stable home environment.

(9)   The quality and continuity of the child's education:

Both parents presented evidence claiming to support the superiority of the schools in their respective neighborhoods. Dr. Rosenstein noted that the father intended to remain in his current home indefinitely, and that if the mother eventually moved out of her parents' home, that could result in a school change.

The court finds no significant difference between the respective schools or any significant differences in the probable quality and continuity of the child's education in either home.

(10)   The fitness of the parents:

Based on the testimony and documentary evidence, the court finds that both parents are fit and financially stable, and that both greatly love and care for the child.

(11)   The geographical proximity of the parents' homes:

The current distance between the parents' homes is approximately 90 miles, a drive of one and a half to two and a half hours, depending upon traffic conditions. Both experts agree that the distance is the primary barrier to a 50/50 shared-parenting arrangement.

(12)   The extent and quality of the time spent with the child prior to or subsequent to the separation:

The parents have generally split both time and parenting responsibilities equally. The mother has recently spent somewhat more time with the child, but the father notes that this was not by agreement, and alleges that it reflects her unwillingness to continue to treat him as an equal parent, without cause.

Based on the father's uncontroverted testimony, the court finds that the mother has recently had more time with the child only due to her interference with the previous agreement.

(13)   The parents' employment responsibilities:

Dr. Hagerty found that the parents' employment responsibilities were similar, and that any differences were not relevant. Dr. Rosenstein, however, noted that the father's schedule was currently much more flexible.

Based on the testimony and documentary evidence, the court finds that both parents have employment responsibilities that are predictable, consistent, and stable, and that would permit them to care for the child and meet her needs. The father's schedule, however, is somewhat more flexible, which would allow him to drop off and pick up the child from school on most days.

The Court's Conclusions and Custody Order

After stating the above findings, the court concluded that the parents should share legal custody, but that Ryan would be designated as primary residential parent. This decision was based primarily on the findings regarding Factor 1, "the parent's ability to agree, communicate and cooperate in matters relating to the child;" Factor 2, "the parents' willingness to accept custody and any history of unwillingness to allow parenting time not based on substantiated abuse;" Factor 11, "the geographical proximity of the parents' homes;" and Factor 13, "the parents' employment responsibilities."

The court ordered the parents to implement the schedule recommended by Dr. Rosenstein at the beginning of the coming academic year. The order also incorporated Dr. Hagerty's suggestion regarding daily calls, while cautioning the parents that during such calls they must take care not to upset the child's peace or stability and must refrain from disparaging the other parent in any way.

This schedule, the court reasoned, would give both mother and father frequent and continuing contact with the child, while avoiding undue stress on the child from too frequent travel. If either parent opted to move and reduce the distance between the homes, the mother could request more equal time. The court pointed out that even the alternate weekend schedule could become burdensome over time given the current distance between the homes, particularly as the child became more involved in extracurricular activities. The parents were free to modify the schedule by mutual agreement as it pertained to pick up and drop off times or specific dates, but neither of them was to change the current split of parenting time without a written agreement signed by both parties, or a court order to the contrary.

Chapter 5

Modifying and Enforcing Parenting Orders

Most post-judgment child custody and visitation issues occur because:

- *one party fails to carry out the orders of the court, or*
- *a change of circumstances justifies a modification of the court's orders.*

New Jersey courts retain the authority to modify child custody orders or enter related orders until all children covered by the orders are emancipated. In New Jersey, "emancipation" relates to a child's financial independence from parents, and it can depend on several factors. You can find a more complete discussion of emancipation later in this book.

Modifying Parenting Orders

A parent applying for modification of a parenting order must prove that circumstances have changed substantially since the date of the original decision. Usually the change must already have occurred and must be expected to continue indefinitely or for at least a lengthy period of time. As with original parenting plans, New Jersey courts expect parents to make their best efforts to work out an acceptable new plan through negotiation or mediation prior to asking for court intervention. Any factor impacting the child's best interests is relevant to the request for change.

Relocation Cases

One of the most difficult situations for separated or divorced families arises when one parent decides to move away from the area and wants to take the children to the new location. Employment related relocation is common in today's economy. Many divorced parents also wish to move closer to extended family members who live out of state and can provide financial and/or emotional support. Some parents remarry a new spouse who works a considerable distance away.

The parent of a minor child born in New Jersey cannot move out of state with the child unless the other parent agrees or a court determines that the relocation is permissible. Sometimes parents agree that one of them needs to relocate, and they work out a new agreement allowing the moving parent to remove the child from the state. This can then be formalized in court with a consent order. More commonly, one parent opposes the move. The parent who wishes to move with the child must then file a motion in Family Court and obtain a court order granting removal. Whether or not the court will allow the child to move with the parent depends on many factors. The analysis will differ depending on the type of custody arrangement currently in effect.

Relocation Cases without Custody Orders

Parents who have separated without custody orders, or who are still living together with their child, are sometimes taken by surprise when the other parent takes the child on a purportedly temporary trip, and then simply does not return. Separated parents can guard against this by obtaining temporary custody and visitation orders as soon as possible. If do you find yourself caught in this situation, take action immediately to obtain orders that will protect your child and your relationship with your child. Courts do not look kindly on parents who intentionally interfere with the relationship between a child and the other parent, and will likely order the absent parent to return with the child. Parents who disregard such an order leave themselves open to parental kidnapping charges. If you are considering filing kidnapping charges against the other parent, consult a family law attorney first. This is a drastic accusation that ensures escalating conflict.

There are certain situations, usually relating to domestic violence, where a court will agree that a parent needed to leave with the child for self-protection or protection of the child. Mothers are not the only parents who can become victims of domestic violence. If you are a father who legitimately fears that your child's other parent may harm you or your child, you can visit Weinberger Divorce and Family Law Group's website for free information about domestic violence, including detailed

94

instructions on how to file a restraining order. If either you or your child is in physical danger, do not hesitate to take action. Call the police or go to the police station and take the children with you. You can also contact a Domestic Violence Shelter or a New Jersey domestic violence attorney for immediate assistance.

If you do not have a parenting agreement and you suspect that your child's other parent may be planning to leave with the children, contact an attorney immediately for assistance. You will need to file a motion in Family Court as soon as possible.

Relocating with Custody Orders

The law has shifted back and forth in recent years regarding the burden on parents - whether mothers or fathers - who wish to move away with children. Prior to the 2001 case of Baures v. Lewis, 167 N.J. 91, New Jersey law required even a parent with primary residential custody to show a real advantage tied to the move (*Cooper v. Cooper*, 99 NJ 42, 1984). The *Baures* case changed the law to provide that a custodial parent wishing to relocate with a child need only produce evidence that:

- the parent had a "good faith" reason for the move—meaning essentially any reason that was genuine and not motivated by a desire to keep the child away from the other parent, and
- the move would not be harmful to the child - meaning that educational and recreational opportunities in the new location are at least comparable to those in the original location, and that a new visitation plan would allow the child to maintain a close relationship with the non-custodial parent.

The presumption afforded the custodial parent under *Baures* did not apply where parents shared legal and physical custody. "Shared custody" means equal or nearly equal parenting time and equal division of the day-to-day responsibilities of parenting. In shared custody arrangements, a court would hold a full hearing on the question of whether or not it would be in the child's best interests to change the parenting arrangement to designate the moving parent as the parent of primary residence. If the court found that it was, the *Baures* analysis would apply.

Baures was the law in New Jersey for about 16 years, but it has recently changed once again, and rather dramatically. In the August 2017 case *Bisbing v. Bisbing*, the New Jersey Supreme Court declared that any parent wishing to move out of state with a child must present an argument for modification of parenting orders based on a substantial change in circumstances, and must demonstrate that the proposed change would be in the child's best interests rather than simply not harmful to the child.

The *Bisbing* court reexamined the requirements of N.J.S.A. 9:2-2. This statute states that a divorced or separated parent must demonstrate "cause" before moving out of New Jersey with a child who was born in the state, or who has lived in the state for at least five years, over the objection of the other parent, or the objection of the child if the child is old enough.

The court cited two pre-*Baures* cases, *Cooper v. Cooper*, and *Holder v. Polanski*, 111 NJ 344 (1988), for the proposition that "cause" was included in the statute "to preserve the rights of the noncustodial parent and the child to main and develop their familial relationship." *Baures*, as the court discussed, significantly reduced the burden on the custodial parent to demonstrate cause. The rationale for this was current social science research closely linking positive post-divorce adjustment of children with the psychological well-being of their custodial parents. Since the psychological well-being of a custodial parent would generally be improved by the ability to pursue career and relationship opportunities without undue geographical constraint, it followed that children would indirectly benefit from allowing a parent to do this.

At the time *Baure* was decided, the supporting social science research appeared to be driving a trend in favor of easing restrictions on custodial parents wishing to move with their children. The *Bisbing* court pointed out, however, that since the *Baure* decision, the trend has lost ground, as the underlying research had received both criticism and support. While no research controverts the idea that the happiness of custodial parents is linked to the happiness of children, other research has shown that relocating far from one parent can negatively affect a child. Other research also shows that the quality of a child's relationship with a noncustodial father is important to the child's well-being. Still other research shows that children can suffer negative effects when either parent moves far away, regardless of which parent makes the move and whether or not the child also moves (*Bisbing v. Bisbing*).

Another reason the *Bisbing* court offered for the change in the law was a concern that the *Baures* rule had perhaps engendered unnecessary disputes between parents over which of them would receive the designation of parent of primary residence, thereby gaining an edge in any future litigation over a move-away.

Bisbing can be considered something of a victory for father's rights in divorce, as more mothers than fathers are still custodial parents, or parents of primary residence.

On the other hand, of course, if you are a father with primary custody and you are thinking about moving, this decision could make things more challenging for you. In either case, fathers desiring to move with children or desiring to challenge a move by the other parent must consider the factors in the custody statute. The best interests standards will still take into account each parent's relationship with a child and each parent's past and current assumption of responsibilities, irrespective of parenting time. The best interests factors are discussed in detail above, in "How Courts Make Custody Decisions."

General Considerations in Relocation Cases

Whether you are a father opposing a move-away, or a father who wants to move away with your child, the best approach is to focus on your child's needs and how your proposed parenting plan will meet those needs. When parents live a considerable distance from one another, courts usually require children to spend large blocks of time with both the primary parent and the alternate parent. This often means that the child will spend the school year in one location and at least the summer and winter vacations in another.

Both parents must be aware that contested relocation cases are often time-consuming and expensive. The court may appoint a mental health professional to evaluate the potential effects of a proposed move on the child as well as the adequacy of proposed alternative visitation plans. Sometimes parents who disagree with the evaluator's opinion wish to hire their own custody experts. This can be extremely expensive and will not always improve the parent's chances. If each parent hires an expert, the opinions sometimes end up cancelling each other out. Before you consider hiring any expert, be sure to thoroughly familiarize yourself with the expert's previous opinions. Your attorney can give you additional information regarding the necessity of hiring experts and the type of expert that might be helpful to your case.

Finally, any parent dealing with a relocation situation should be aware that changes in this area of the law have been relatively frequent in recent years. To be certain of the current state of the law, you should always consult a family law attorney.

Enforcing Parenting Orders

Parents have a legal duty to comply with court-ordered parenting plans. In most cases, this duty includes encouraging a child to spend time with the other parent. On the one hand, parents need to maintain a certain degree of flexibility to make a plan work; running off to court after every minor violation of the terms is not conducive to peaceful co-parenting. On the other hand, consistent or extreme violations may be best addressed through legal channels.

Interference with custody or visitation includes not only total prevention of contact between a child and a parent, but also subtler behavior such as blocking telephone or email contact, or consistently scheduling a child's appointments and activities during the other parent's scheduled visitation time. Even talking about the other parent in a negative manner is a form of interference. Children are very impressionable; hearing one parent continually complain about the other can deeply affect the parent-child relationship. Taken to the extreme, such actions can constitute "parental alienation." Parental alienation is discussed above, under "How Courts Make Custody Decisions."

If you find yourself in a situation where your child's other parent is consistently violating the court's orders regarding custody and visitation, you may want to bring both a motion to enforce litigant's rights and a motion requesting a change in the parenting arrangements. An attorney can help you decide which motion or motions would be necessary and appropriate.

Remedies for Interference:

A judge who finds that a child is refusing to spend time with one parent due to behavior of the other has the authority to order whatever remedies are justified under the individual circumstances. The judge can impose penalties on the interfering parent, and may consider whether the child's best interests would be served by changing the current parenting arrangement, either temporarily or permanently, including potentially changing the primary residential parent.

In an appropriate case, a court might order some or all of the following:

- compensatory parenting time for the parent who has lost time,

- changes in transportation arrangements for visitation,

- changes in the children's pick-up location, or

- a change in the primary residential parent.

A court might also order additional penalties, including ordering the interfering parent to:

- pay the other parent's attorney's fees and court costs,

- attend parenting classes or counseling,

- pay for counseling for the children or for the other parent,

- pay any costs resulting from non-compliance with court orders,

- participate in community service, or

- comply with a warrant for arrest.

See New Jersey Court Rule 5:3-7.

Interfering with court-ordered parenting time is serious and can even be a crime in New Jersey. A parent who conceals a child from the other parent for the purpose of interfering with custody or visitation may have to serve jail time. If you suspect that your child's other parent may be planning to leave the area with the children, contact an attorney immediately for assistance. You will need to file a motion in Family Court as soon as possible. If the other parent has already left the state with the children without providing you with contact information, do not hesitate to call the police as well. The sooner you get help trying to locate the children, the more likely it is that they will be located without delay.

Defenses to Interference:

In some cases, a parent will have a legitimate defense to a charge of interference with parenting time. This includes situations where a parent is attempting to escape from the other parent's imminent violence, or where a parent believes that their child is in imminent danger from the other parent. A parent asserting this kind of defense must, as soon as possible, and always within 24 hours of leaving the area with the child, contact DCP&P (1 (855) INFO DCF), the local police, or the district attorney's office in the child's county of primary residence, and reveal the child's new location. A parent fleeing from domestic violence can also bring a custody action in an appropriate court as soon as reasonably possible.

If you believe that your situation entitles you to a defense against charges of interference with custody or visitation, do not risk making yourself vulnerable to such charges; contact an attorney or DCP&P to ensure that you are complying with the law.

Failure to Receive Child Support Payments:

Parents who are not receiving timely child support payments sometimes feel justified in blocking the non-paying parent's access to the child. This is not acceptable under New Jersey law. The purpose of child support is to cover expenses for children while they are with the other parent. It is not paid in exchange for visitation rights. If the other parent is denying your visitation rights, you can file a motion in court to enforce those rights. The court will not prevent you from seeing your child if you are not up-to-date in child support payments, but you may find yourself subject to penalties for nonpayment. There is more information on enforcement of child support later in this book.

Failure to Exercise Parenting Time:

If your child's other parent consistently fails to exercise parenting time, you can ask the court to modify your parenting schedule based on a substantial change in circumstances. You can then also ask for a modification of your child support order to reflect the reality of the situation. A parent who spends little time with a child is reasonably expected to pay more child support to cover the cost of things such as additional meals or caregivers to cover the absence of the second parent.

Case Studies: Enforcing and Modifying New Jersey Child Custody Orders

1.   Modifying a Parenting Agreement in a Move-away Case

For three years after their divorce, Chris and Rachel co-parented together with little conflict. They lived less than five miles apart from one another in Cherry Hill, New Jersey, and were therefore easily able to alternate weeks with their children. Lisa, a quiet and serious girl who was also a star student, was now almost 14 and would soon be starting high school. Kyle, who at 10 years old was more outgoing than his sister and already a talented and dedicated soccer player, would be entering 5th grade next year, the last grade in his current elementary school.

Chris was stunned when Rachel told him she had accepted a promotion at work that would require her to move her office to Manhattan. She had found a house in Glen Ridge, New Jersey, approximately 84 miles from Cherry Hill, and she wanted the children to relocate there with her before the beginning of the next school year. In consultation with an attorney, she had come up with a proposed new parenting schedule that she believed would allow Chris to continue to spend as much time as possible with the kids after the move. The children would be with him for 8 weeks in the summer, one week each during winter and spring breaks, and one weekend per month (Friday evening through Sunday evening) during the school year.

Chris strongly objected. He pointed out that this plan would cut his parenting time nearly in half. He also told Rachel that he did not think the children would want to move to a new neighborhood. He asked her not to say anything to them before he'd had a chance to consult with his own attorney.

Chris's attorney, Marie Holbrook, told him that if Rachel was committed to moving that far away, they would have to come up with a revised parenting schedule. There was no reason, however, that Rachel should automatically have the right to enroll the children in school in her new neighborhood. A judge would look at all of the factors in the New Jersey child custody statute to determine what kind of new arrangement would be best for the children. If there were no significant advantages or disadvantages either way, Chris could at least argue that since they currently shared time equally, and Rachel was the one deciding to move, her proposed schedule should be reversed, giving Chris 75% of parenting time and Rachel 25%.

There was also another factor to consider, Ms. Holbrook pointed out. Lisa, at nearly 14, was old enough to have her own thoughts and feelings taken into account. Since Kyle was only 10, he was not necessarily entitled to a vote, but it would undoubtedly be helpful to his parents to know his thoughts and feelings as well.

"Finding out how kids really feel can be tricky," Ms. Holbrook noted. "Even if parents normally have a good rapport with their children and maintain open lines of communication, it's a different story when the kids land in the middle of a dispute between the parents. Kids often won't spontaneously express an opinion one way or another because they don't want to hurt either parent's feelings. It's a real dilemma for them."

Ms. Holbrook then suggested that Chris and Rachel consider hiring a joint child specialist to interview the children. "The specialist would also meet with both of you," she told him, "and would consider all the circumstances in your case. You could then get a written report, or the specialist could attend a mediation session with you and Rachel. If at all possible, you will want to avoid bringing this into a courtroom. Once you start hiring separate experts and attending court hearings, things can get very expensive very quickly. Since you two have been so successful at co-parenting so far, I don't see any reason you couldn't resolve this in mediation."

Chris met with Rachel and expressed his opinion that since she was the one moving, her proposed new schedule should be flipped so that the kids could stay in their current schools. As he had anticipated, Rachel did not agree. She pointed out that she had spent a long time choosing a neighborhood with good schools and other resources that would support the children in their favorite pursuits. Chris then shared Ms. Holbrook's suggestion that they hire a child specialist together. Rachel agreed that this was a good idea. She said that she would have her attorney contact Ms. Holbrook to come up with a mutual recommendation.

After the parents had agreed on a child specialist, they sat down together with Lisa and Kyle to share the news that Rachel was relocating. They also shared their plan for all of them to meet with the specialist to help Chris and Rachel come up with a new parenting plan. "Both of us are going to do everything in our power," Chris assured the kids, "to find the arrangement that will be best for you."

Much to the surprise of both parents, Lisa immediately stated that she didn't need to talk to anybody; she already knew that she wanted to go Glen Ridge with her mother. "No offense to you Dad, but both of you know what a bad year I've had at school with the whole 'mean girls' crew. If I go to high school with them next year, it will just be more of the same. A chance to start over in a new neighborhood would be a dream come true for me. Plus, Glen Ridge is so close to New York City. I would love that."

Upon hearing this, Kyle burst into tears. "I don't want to move!" he exclaimed. "All my friends are here! And I don't want Mom and Lisa to move away either!"

Fortunately, the whole family was able to calm Kyle down by assuring him that whatever new arrangement they came up with, they would make sure that he continued to see both of his parents and his sister as much as possible. They were not going to make any final decisions yet, they assured him.

After the family meeting, the shaken parents conferred about their next steps. They agreed to go ahead and schedule the meetings with the child specialist. Both of them felt they needed more input to be sure that they were keeping the children's best interests in the forefront. They also both began to think that maybe they needed to come up with a more creative plan than either of them had thought of so far.

During the next few weeks everyone in the family met with the specialist. Rachel also took Lisa and Kyle separately to see the house she would be moving into and to tour the neighborhood. After that, the parents attended a mediation session with a private mediator that they chose together, and eventually, they came up with the following plan:

Lisa would live primarily with Rachel and Kyle would live primarily with Jim. They would reassess this plan next year before Kyle started middle school, and then again in four years before he started high school. For the time being, both kids would be with Rachel on the first weekend of each month and with Chris on the third weekend. They would each spend the second and fourth weekends at their primary homes (Lisa with Rachel and

Kyle with Chris). All other breaks, including winter, spring and summer would be split roughly in half between the parents, and the children would move between the two homes together. Both parents agreed to be flexible with weekend time to accommodate the children's extracurricular activities, as well as to make sure that any three or four-day weekend holidays would be divided equally between them. They also agreed to maintain at all times a primary goal of keeping the kids together as much as possible.

While neither Chris nor Rachel was 100% happy with the new plan, they both agreed that it was the best possible solution under all of the circumstances. They agreed to file their plan with the court as a consent order, avoiding any further conflict or additional legal expenses.

2.   Enforcing Parenting Orders and Seeking Remedies for Noncompliance

Jim had had just about enough of Karen's antics. According to their court-ordered parenting plan, Jessica, age 8, and Tony, age 5, were to spend three nights every other weekend with Jim. For the fourth time in only three months, however, Karen had refused to comply with the schedule. She claimed that the kids had colds and needed to stay home. Jim told her that they could rest at his place as easily as at hers, but she refused to budge. When he asked to speak to them on the phone, she said they were sleeping. For Jim, it was the last straw. Lately Karen had come up with one excuse after another to keep the kids away from him. To make matters worse, the last time they did spend the weekend, Tony had blurted out, "Mommy says you aren't a good dad, and that you're mean, and you drink too much!"

Horrified at Tony's outburst, Jim had looked at Jessica. She was a little older, he thought, so maybe she knew what this was all about, but should he ask her? It didn't seem quite right. She chimed in on her own though, "It's true, Daddy. Mommy says mean things about you all the time. Also, I heard her tell Grandma that you let us eat junk food for dinner, and that every time we come back from your house, we're filthy and my hair is a tangled rat's nest."

Jim was appalled. None of this was true - except maybe, he conceded to himself, the part about Jessica's hair. Silently he pledged to try harder with that. At the same time, though, he felt his rage growing at the way Karen had been treating him. It wasn't right, he thought, and it couldn't be good for the kids either. He wasn't sure what to do about it though, especially since he and Karen were barely on speaking terms.

After some thought, Jim decided to send Karen an email. He had already sent her one email a few weeks ago complaining about her noncompliance with the schedule, but obviously that had not been enough. This time he listed every occasion during the past year that she had refused to let the kids see him. He told her that she needed to start complying with the schedule and to stop saying derogatory things about him to the children. He even sent her a couple of articles by respected child development professionals, documenting the harm to children that could result when one parent denigrated the other in front of them.

Unfortunately, Karen just ignored Jim's email. When she made up another excuse to cancel one of his weekends the following month, Jim decided it was time for him to contact an attorney. A friend recommended Olivia Hunt, an experienced family lawyer. When Jim shared with

Ms. Hunt the extreme degree to which Karen had failed to follow the parenting schedule, along with the things the children had told him she'd said, the attorney recommended that he file both a motion to enforce his parenting rights and a motion requesting a change in the parenting arrangements. A judge who found that the kids were not spending court-ordered time with him because of Karen's interference, Ms. Hunt explained, could order compensatory parenting time to make up for the weekends he had missed. If he requested it, he might even get an order making him the primary residential parent instead of Karen. He could also ask the court to order Karen to pay his attorney's fees and court costs. Ms. Hunt suggested that he also request that Karen be ordered to attend parenting classes or counseling, and if necessary, to pay for counseling for the children to protect them from a potential pattern of parental alienation.

When Karen received the motion from Jim and his attorney, she responded by filing a declaration accusing Jim of various lapses in good parenting. Her accusations included the things Tony and Jessica had listed - that Jim fed the children junk food, didn't see that they bathed, and drank heavily while he was with them. Fortunately for Jim, these allegations were all untrue, and Karen had no support for any of them. Instead, they only served to alienate the presiding judge.

After a brief hearing on Jim's motions, the judge ordered a temporary change in the parenting schedule. The children were to spend three weekends per month with Jim until all of the missed weekends had been made up. The judge also ordered Karen to attend parenting classes and to pay 80% of Jim's attorney's fees for the court motions. Although the judge did not permanently change the parenting schedule, he did add two provisions to the existing parenting orders: The first stated that Karen must allow Jim to have one 30-minute phone or skype call with the kids each night. The second ordered both parents to refrain from denigrating each other in the children's presence. Finally, the judge issued a stern warning to Karen, advising her that if she continued to interfere with the relationship between Jim and the children, she would lose her status as primary residential parent.

Chapter 6

New Jersey Child Support Guidelines

After child custody, the legal topic of greatest importance to separated or divorced fathers is usually child support. Fathers sometimes assume that courts will hold them (as opposed to mothers) primarily responsible for supporting children financially. In New Jersey, however, both mothers and fathers are required to contribute to the costs of raising children according to their earning ability. New Jersey child support amounts are based on each parent's income and the amount of time each parent spends with a child. A parent who is unemployed or underemployed can be attributed with additional income (known as "imputation" of income) to ensure an appropriate level of contribution.

If your child's other parent is the higher earner, you may wonder if that means you will not have to pay child support, or even that you might receive child support from the other parent. Again, in New Jersey, regardless of which party is the higher earner, both parents are always required to contribute to the costs of raising a child. If you earn significantly less than the other parent, however, it is possible, depending on all of the circumstances, that you could receive child support payments. One parent usually ends up paying the other some net amount of support.

New Jersey Child Support Guidelines (Guidelines) are clear but complex. Parents on either end of a child support request will benefit from understanding them. They consist of more than 100 pages of detailed explanation, instructions, forms and charts, and are based on extensive research and evaluation into the most equitable ways to hold parents responsible for meeting children's financial needs. The current version is contained in Appendix IX to Court Rule 5:6A. Parents without on-line access can obtain a copy from a family law attorney or from the law library at any New Jersey courthouse.

Parents with well-defined parenting arrangements can estimate the child support a court might order by consulting the Guidelines and completing the applicable worksheets. Parents with less well-defined arrangements may need to work on their parenting plan before they can use the worksheets effectively. In constructing a plan, it is important to keep in mind that determination of child support is not connected with legal custody of children, but only with the division of parenting time and with which parent pays actual direct costs of child support.

This book provides a general overview the current Guidelines. More information is available from the Guidelines themselves, or from our companion e-book in this series, "New Jersey Child Support." If you still have questions after consulting these resources, a New Jersey family law attorney may be able to provide more information about how courts have interpreted the law in situations similar to your own.

<u>Underlying Research and Assumptions of the New Jersey Child Support Guidelines</u>

New Jersey courts follow the "Income Shares Model" of child support. Under this model, courts set child support amounts by beginning with the approximate amount that parents would spend on a child in an intact two-parent family with a similar income level, and then splitting this amount between the parents in proportion to their respective incomes. So, for example, if one parent earns 70% of the total income that parent is assigned 70% of the total award.

The formula set out in the New Jersey Child Support Guidelines governs payment of temporary or permanent child support in any contested or uncontested action, unless a party demonstrates that the circumstances of a specific case make application of the Guidelines inappropriate or unfair. In any such case, the court will go back to the underlying statutory factors set out in the New Jersey child support statute (NJSA 2A:34-23). Those factors are listed later in this book. A court that orders a non-guideline support amount must state the reasons for the deviation in writing. Parents can agree to a deviation, but they must state their reasons in a Marital Settlement Agreement. Common situations calling for Guideline deviations are further discussed below.

Appendix IX-A to New Jersey Court Rule 5:6A contains an in-depth explanation of the philosophy, economic principles and general assumptions that underlie the Guidelines. Appendix IX-B contains additional explanations, as well as line by line instructions for completing the Guideline worksheets. In many cases parents may be able to avoid arguments over child support simply by familiarizing themselves with both Appendix IX-A and Appendix IX-B.

Appendix IX-F (Schedule of Child Support Awards) sets out average costs of raising children according to bracketed income levels. Amounts include the following:

- **Fixed expenses**. These include housing costs, such as rent or mortgage and utility payments. The current guidelines assume that fixed expenses equal 38% of total child care costs.

- **Controlled expenses.** These include the cost of items such as clothing, personal care products or services, most entertainment and most miscellaneous items. The current guidelines assume that "controlled" expenses constitute 25% of total costs.

- **Variable expenses**. These include expenditures within the control of the parent with whom the child is currently staying, such as food, transportation, and occasional entertainment. The current guidelines assume that variable costs equal 37% of total costs.

The Sole Parenting and Shared Parenting Worksheets

Either parent can estimate the amount of child support a New Jersey judge would be likely to order by completing the appropriate worksheet. The basic formula is set out in Appendix IX-C (Sole Parenting Worksheet). In a shared parenting situation, where children's time with each parent exceeds approximately 28% of overnight time, a court has discretion to use the shared parenting formula set out in Appendix IX-D (Shared Parenting Worksheet). "Shared parenting" is further defined as at least 104 overnights per year, with an "overnight," consisting of at least a 12-hour period of time. Parents are required to file one of these worksheets with the court in any New Jersey Family Division case establishing or modifying support.

Both the Sole Parenting Worksheet and the Shared Parenting Worksheet begin with a calculation of each parent's net income. We will look more closely at income calculations in the next section. After each parent's income has been calculated, the incomes are added together to obtain an appropriate child support amount from Appendix IX-F. This amount is then allocated between the parents based on their percentage share of the total income. The amount allocated to each parent based on income is then further adjusted based on the percentage of time a child spends in each parent's household.

The Sole Parenting Worksheet allows a parenting time adjustment for **variable expenses** only, while the Shared Parenting Worksheet also allows an additional adjustment for the higher **fixed expenses** required to maintain a secondary residence for the child. The result of these adjustments is that the total cost of child support will be higher under the Shared Parenting Worksheet. Due to the priority of first ensuring that children have an adequate primary residence, courts will not apply a shared parenting formula unless the parents meet certain minimum income requirements.

Regardless of whether the sole parenting or shared parenting formula is used, the guidelines assume that the custodial parent or parent of primary residence (PPR) will be required to purchase virtually all items included in **controlled expenses**, and that the parent of alternate residence (PAR) will not have to duplicate such items. Controlled expenses are therefore not adjusted for parenting time, but only according to the parents' respective incomes. In an appropriate case, where, for example, parenting time is exactly equal and it is necessary to duplicate many controlled expenses, the parents could agree to an additional adjustment, or the PAR could request such an adjustment from the court.

Both worksheets provide for the addition of certain supplemental expenses. Various additional adjustments may also be appropriate under certain circumstances. We discuss supplemental expenses and other adjustments in detail below.

After making all applicable adjustments, the non-custodial parent or PAR will usually pay a percentage of the total award to the custodial parent or PPR. The PPR's or custodial parent's share is assumed to be expended directly on costs associated with child-rearing. In a shared parenting situation, depending on each parent's income and the amount of time children spend with each parent, either parent could end up paying support to the other.

Calculating Income Available for Support

Gross and Net Income:

Guideline child support in New Jersey is based on the combined net income—gross income minus allowable deductions—of both parents. Gross income includes most types of earned or unearned income. Appendix IX-B contains an in-depth explanation of what a court will ordinarily include as available gross income. Self-employment, business or rent/royalty income is calculated as gross receipts minus "ordinary and necessary expenses" of generating the receipts. The allowable business expenses are limited to those listed in Appendix IX-B.

If a parent has sporadic or fluctuating income such as income from seasonal work, dividends, commissions, or bonuses, gross income will usually be determined by averaging the amount of the income over the previous 36 months, or from the time it was first received, whichever time period is shorter. Overtime or second job income is averaged only for the most recent 12-month period. A parent who has sporadic income that is not expected to continue into the future can ask the court not to include it. An allowance for housing or meals, such as a military allowance for quarters or subsistence, is included, as is the value of any employment benefits that reduce personal living expenses—such as subsidized housing, meals, or a company car.

Non-taxable income must be listed separately from taxable income, as a withholding allowance is calculated based on the taxable income only.

Excluded Income:
A few types of income are specifically excluded from gross income. These include means-tested (income based) public assistance benefits such as Temporary Assistance to Needy Families, Supplemental Security Income and the value of food stamps; mandatory nontaxable retirement contributions; child support a parent receives for children from another relationship; and the net amount of alimony or spousal maintenance a parent pays to a current or former spouse. If one parent will be paying alimony to the other in connection with a current divorce, with the exception of pendente lite (temporary) alimony,

the alimony amount should be determined first so that it can be included in the income of the receiving parent and excluded from the income of the paying parent. Parents who are currently going through a divorce should be aware that as part of recent changes to the federal tax code, a spouse paying alimony pursuant to an order or agreement executed after December 31, 2018 will no longer be able to deduct such payments from taxable income. Always be sure to use the most up-to-date versions of rules and worksheets to avoid any potential mischaracterization of income. Appendix IX- B contains some additional less common examples of income that may sometimes be excluded from gross income.

Government benefits that one parent receives specifically for support of children (such as income replacement benefits for disability or retirement, or other non means-tested benefits) are not included in income of the receiving parent, but the amount of the benefit will normally be deducted from the Basic Child Support Award. In a situation where the custodial parent or PPR is disabled and the deduction of the benefit from the PAR or non-custodial parent's support obligation would create a hardship in the child's primary household, the court may adjust or disallow the deduction.

Deductions from Gross Taxable Income:

Allowable deductions from gross taxable income include income taxes, mandatory union dues, and support that a parent pays for children of other relationships. If you have dependents from another relationship (legal or adopted children under age 18) that live with you, you may be able to deduct an amount for support of those dependents as well. You must ask the court to allow this deduction, and you will have to provide the income of the dependent's other parent and complete a separate Sole Parenting Worksheet for that alternate family. This adjustment requires three support calculations—a theoretical support amount for the dependents in the alternate family, a support amount that includes the other-dependent deduction, and a support amount that does not include the other-dependent deduction. Appendix IX-B details the calculations. Additional examples of possible deductions from gross income are also listed in Appendix IX-B.

Verifying Income:

Courts require parties to a child support hearing to submit either a Family Part Case Information Statement (Court Rule 5:5-2) or a Financial Statement in Summary Support Actions (Court Rule 5:5-3) as verification of income. Courts determining gross income before June 30th of the current year will base findings primarily on federal and state income tax returns and supporting documents from the preceding year, such as W-2's and 1099's. Courts determining income after June 30th will use year-to-date income from all available documented sources, including paystubs, employer wage verifications, or statements of business receipts and expenses.

Imputing Income:

If the court finds that either parent is voluntarily unemployed or underemployed, the court will estimate the parent's potential earning capacity in light of factors such as work history, training, education, and available jobs in the area, and may calculate child support based on such income. This kind of calculation may require expert testimony from a vocational evaluator. If a probable income cannot be determined, the calculation will be based on hypothetical full-time employment (40 hours per week) at New Jersey minimum wage ($8.60 per hour as of January 2018).

In deciding whether or not unemployment or underemployment is voluntary, the court will consider the reasons for it; the probable employment status of the parent in an intact two-parent family; the availability of alternate assets for support; the presence of children in the household; and all available child-care options. A parent caring for young children is entitled to an offset for any child care expenses that would be necessary to work.

Adding Supplemental Expenses

After calculating a basic support obligation according to the appropriate parenting worksheet, a court may add certain predictable and recurrent expenses to the award. These include the cost (after any applicable tax credits) of necessary work-related child care, a parent's marginal (additional) cost of adding a child to a health insurance policy, and any predictable and recurring unreimbursed health care expenses exceeding $250 per child per year. These expenses are apportioned to the parents according to their respective incomes, and a parent who pays the expenses directly will receive a credit. Health care expenses that exceed $250 per child per year but are not predictable and recurring are not added to the child support order, but are shared by the parents in proportion to their relative incomes as they are incurred.

Case Studies: Child Support Calculations

1. Example of a Child Support Calculation Using the Sole Parenting Worksheet

Heidi and Jake have been married for nine years and have two children, Sam, 5 and Jenna, 7. Heidi is a business travel manager at an upscale hotel. She works full time and earns approximately $75,000 per year. Jake is a physical therapy assistant and currently earns $28 per hour. He worked 40 hours per week until Jenna was born. For the past two years, he has worked 10 hour shifts on Wednesdays and alternate weekends (Saturdays and Sundays), for an average of 20 hours per week. This schedule has allowed him to be with the children before school every morning, and after school every afternoon except for Wednesdays, when his mother picks them up from school and watches them until one of the parents gets home. Since the kids attend summer camp for about 6 weeks each summer, Jake has also been able to work part-time through the summers without the family incurring additional child care costs.

A few months ago Jake and Heidi separated. Since then, the children have primarily lived with Jake. They spend every other weekend, from Friday night through Sunday night, with Heidi. Heidi also has a floating afternoon or evening activity with each child every week, which she schedules a few days in advance in consultation with Jake. Heidi and Jake have also agreed that Heidi will have the children for two-weeks during summer vacation and for half of all holidays. So far this schedule is working well.

Jake and Heidi decided to attend private mediation to work out their financial issues. When Jake broached the topic of child support, Heidi took issue with his current level of employment. She suggested that since the children were now both in school full-time, Jake could return to working 40 hours a week. "You've always been able to get a flexible schedule," she noted. "If it would help, maybe I could take the kids overnight once or twice a week."

Heidi believed that if Jake returned to work full-time, it would both lower any child support payments she might be responsible for, and also make alimony unnecessary. Jake, however, believed that if he was to work full-time, regardless of whether or not Heidi added in any overnights, the kids would need at least some before and after school care. "You have a lot of evening work events," he pointed out, "My schedule isn't that flexible. Wouldn't the increased child care costs offset any drop in the child support payments?"

After discussing the options for a little while longer, Jake acknowledged that he could probably pick up a couple of 5 hour shifts during the week while the kids were in school. This would increase his hours up to 30 per week without the need for additional child care. He also noted that at 30 hours per week, he would be eligible for employee health insurance. This would be an important benefit for him as he would no longer be eligible for coverage under Heidi's work policy. Her insurance would continue to cover herself and the children, however, who could both remain on her policy for $25 per month.

Jake believed that even if he worked 30 hours per week, he would need some small amount of alimony to make ends meet. If he were to work 40 hours per week, this would probably not be the case. On the other hand, both parents agreed that if Jake worked 40 hours per week, their weekly child care costs would increase from an average of $50 per week (the cost of summer camps averaged out over 52 weeks) to approximately $150 per week.

"This is just getting more confusing, Heidi complained. How are we supposed to weigh out all these different factors?"

"Why don't we run child support calculations for a couple of different scenarios," the mediator suggested. "In the first scenario, Jake would work 40 hours per week with no alimony payments. In the second, he would work 30 hours per week and Heidi would pay a small amount of alimony."

Jake and Heidi agreed to try this, using $50 per week as the hypothetical alimony amount. Heidi then stated that since they had only been married for 9 years, she didn't feel she should have to pay alimony for more than 5 years under any scenario. The mediator noted that in most situations, New Jersey law limited the duration of alimony to no longer than the length of the marriage. "We can talk more about duration," she suggested "after we see what the numbers look like."

A summary of the results of each scenario and a further discussion of options appears after the line by line calculations below. The line references are to the entries required on the Sole Parenting Worksheet, (simplified for purposes of this example). Following the examples line by line on the worksheet may be tedious, but it will also help you understand exactly how the formula works:

<u>Scenario No. 1: Jake works 40 hours per week.</u>

L.1-3: The custodial parent's (Jake's) weekly net taxable income on line 3 is $985 ($1120 in gross income on line 1, minus $135 tax withholding on line 2a). [2]

L.1-3: The non-custodial parent's (Heidi's) weekly net taxable income on line 3 is $1212 ($1442 in gross income on line 1, minus $230 tax withholding on line 2a).

L.6: The total net income for both parents is $2197.

L.7: Jared has approximately 45% of the available income, and Heidi has approximately 55%.

L.8: The basic child support amount for two children with a total parental net income of $2197 is $391 (from <u>App. IX-F</u> Schedules).

L.9: The estimated net cost of work-related child care (after application of a $960 annual tax credit according to <u>App. IX-E</u>) is $150 per week, which is added to the basic support amount.

L.10: The children have health coverage through Heidi's employment at a weekly cost of $25, so this is also added to the basic support amount.

L.13: The total child support amount is $566 per week.

L.14: Jake's income-based share of the support obligation is $255 per week ($566 x 45%); Heidi's share is $311 ($566 x 55%).

---

[2] The tax withholding amounts in both scenarios are approximated for simplicity.

L.16: Heidi would pay the child-care costs, reducing her support obligation by $150 per week.

L.17: Heidi also receives a credit for the $25 per week insurance premium that is deducted from her pay.

L. 20: Jake and Heidi agree that Heidi's current parenting time is equivalent to about 25% (line 20b). To make the adjustment for Heidi's variable expenses during her parenting time, the basic child support amount before adjustments on line 8 ($391) is multiplied by 25% and then by 37%. The resulting amount is rounded to $36, which is an additional credit for Heidi.

L.21: The net child support obligation is $100 a week. This equals Heidi's income-based share of the support obligation ($311) minus the credits for health insurance ($25) and child care payments ($150) minus the adjustment for parenting time ($36).

Heidi would pay $100 in child support to Jake. As the custodial parent, Jake is assumed to pay his share of child-care expenses directly. What Heidi actually ends up paying is $100 (net child support) plus $25 (health insurance premiums) plus $150 (childcare), or $275. Her final income would be $937, which is her net income of $1212, minus her total payments of $275. Jared's final income would be $1085 per week, consisting of his net taxable income of $985 plus a child support payment of $100.

Scenario No. 2: Jake works 30 hours per week.

L.1-3: The custodial parent's (Jared's) weekly net taxable income on line 3 is $790 ($840 in gross income on line 1, plus $50 in alimony on line 1c, minus $100 tax withholding on line 2a).

L.1-3: The non-custodial parent's (Heidi's) weekly net taxable income on line 3 is $1167 ($1442 in gross income on line 1, minus $50 in alimony on line 1b, minus $225 in tax withholding on line 2a).

L.6: The total net income for both parents is $1957.

L.7: Jake has approximately 40% of the available income, and Heidi has approximately 60%.

L.8: The basic child support amount for two children with a total parental net income of $1957 is $369 (from App. IX-F Schedules).

L.9: The estimated net cost of work-related child care (after application of a 20% annual tax credit according to App. IX-E) is $50 per week, which is added to the basic support amount.

L.10: The children have health coverage through Heidi's employment, at a weekly cost of $25, so this is also added to the basic support amount.

L.13: The total child support amount is $444 a week.

L.14: Jake's income-based share of the support obligation is $178 per week (40% of $444); Heidi's share is $266 (60% of $444).

L.16: Heidi will pay the child care costs, reducing her support obligation by $50 per week.

L.17: Heidi also receives a credit for the $25 per week insurance premium that is deducted from her pay.

L. 20: Jared and Heidi agree that Heidi's current parenting time is equivalent to about 25% (line 20b). To make the adjustment for Heidi's variable expenses during her parenting time, the basic child support amount before

126

adjustments on line 8 ($369) is multiplied by 25% and then by 37%. This figure is rounded to $34, which is an additional credit for Heidi.

L.21: The net child support obligation is equal to Heidi's income-based share of the support obligation ($266) minus the credits for health insurance ($25) and child care payments ($50) minus the adjustment for parenting time ($34), or $157 per week.

Heidi would pay $157 to Jake. As the custodial parent, Jake is assumed to pay his share of child-care expenses directly. What Heidi ends up paying on this plan is $157 (net child support), plus a net $45 of alimony ($50 minus a $5 tax benefit) plus $25 (health insurance premiums), plus $50 (childcare), or $277. Her final income would be $935, which is her net income of $1167 (including the alimony deduction), minus her additional payments for child support, health insurance and childcare. Jake's net income would include his net taxable income of $790 (which includes $50 in alimony), plus a child support payment of $157, for a total of $947.

Assessing the Options

When Heidi realized that Jake's working 40 hours per week rather than 30 hours would add only $2 to her weekly income, she agreed to pay the $50 in alimony. Jake, on the other hand, realized that the difference between the two plans mainly affected him, as even after allowing for the increased child care costs, he would keep an additional $138 per week if he worked full-time. He decided that at this time, the children would be better off if he continued to work only part-time, but he agreed to reassess this each year. Heidi stated that since there was little financial difference to her, she was willing to pay the

$50 per week of alimony either until Jake decided to go back to work full-time, or until they agreed that the kids no longer needed paid child care, up to a maximum of 9 years. Both of them agreed to re-run the child support calculations whenever there was a s substantial change in circumstances, such as a major change in the parenting schedule or a substantial increase or decrease in income for either of them.

2. Example of a Child Support Calculation Using the Shared Parenting Worksheet

Kayla and Brian recently decided to separate after living together for 10 years without marrying. They have two children together, Nina, age 9, and Lisa, age 7. Brian is an electrical engineer and earns approximately $110,000 per year. Kayla is a librarian at a local college, earning approximately $65,000 per year. Both Brian and Kayla wanted primary custody of the children, but after a brief period of negotiation, they agreed that a parenting plan that matches their current parenting responsibilities as closely as possible would give them nearly equal time and make the most sense.

Kayla works from 7 a.m. to 3 p.m., which permits her to be home at about the same time the children get off of the school bus each day. Brian typically works until 5 or 6 p.m., but he is able to telecommute up to two days per week, which has allowed him to be home often during school holidays or if one of the children was ill. Kayla and Brian decide to try a modified split week schedule. Brian will telecommute on Thursdays and Fridays. He will pick the children up from Kayla's apartment at 5 pm on Wednesdays and Kayla will pick them up from Brian's apartment at 5 pm on Fridays every other week and on Sundays on the alternate weeks. They also agree to share equal time on school holidays, and to make sure that each parent has a two-week stretch with the children each summer so that they can take a vacation together. They work everything out on a calendar, which shows that Kayla will have 190 overnights per year with the children and Brian will have 175.

Although Brian earns substantially more than Kayla, since they never married, there is no alimony issue to decide. They agree to use the Shared Parenting Worksheet, with the following calculations:

L.1-3: The parent of primary residence (PPR/Kayla) has a weekly net taxable income on line 3 of $1030 ($1250 in gross income on line 1, minus $220 tax withholding (simplified) on line 2a).

L.1-3: The parent of alternate residence (PAR/Brian) has a weekly net taxable income on line 3 of $1515 ($2115 in gross income on line 1, minus $600 tax withholding (simplified) on line 2a).

L.6: The total net income for both parents is $2545.

L.7: Brian has approximately 60% of the available income and Kayla has approximately 40%.

L.8: The basic child support amount for two children with a total parental net income of $2545 is $423 (From App. IX-F Schedules).

L.9: Kayla has 190 overnights and Brian has 175.

L.10: Kayla's percentage share of overnights is 52% and Brian's is 48%.

L.11: The PAR shared parenting fixed expenses are $154, which is equal to the basic support amount on line 8

($423) multiplied by Paul's percentage share of overnights (48%), then by 38%, then by 2.

L.12: The shared parenting basic support amount is increased by $154, to $577.

L.13: Brian's share of the shared parenting basic support amount is 60% of $577, or $346. Kayla's share is 40%, or $231.

L.14: The PAR share of variable expenses is Brian's percentage of overnights (48%), multiplied by the basic child support amount of $423, then by 37%, or $75.

L.15: The PAR adjusted shared parenting basic child support amount is Brian's share of the basic support amount on line 13 ($346), minus the PAR share of fixed expenses on line 11 ($154), minus the PAR share of variable expenses on line 14 ($75), or $117.

L.16: The parties do not need child care.

L.17: The children currently have health coverage through Kayla's employment at no additional cost to her.

There are no additional adjustments. Brian will pay Kayla $117 dollars per week to cover his share of expenses for the children while they are in her care. As the PPR, Kayla is assumed to pay her share of child-care expenses directly.

Chapter 7

Deviating from the Child Support Guidelines

Although the guidelines cover the vast majority of cases, there are situations in which a court may order support that varies from the guideline recommendations. Courts have discretion to order a different amount in any situation where a deviation would be in the best interests of a child, provided that the child support order specifies in writing what the amount would have been had the guidelines been followed, and the reason for the deviation.

The New Jersey child support statute requires courts deviating from the Guidelines to consider the statutory factors that form the basis for the Guidelines. These are the following:

- Needs of the child;
- Standard of living and economic circumstances of each parent;
- All sources of income and assets of each parent;
- Earning ability of each parent, including educational background, training, employment skills, work experience, custodial responsibility for children including the cost of providing child care and the length of time and cost of each parent to obtain training or experience for appropriate employment;
- Need and capacity of the child for education, including higher education;
- Age and health of the child and each parent;
- Income, assets and earning ability of the child;
- Responsibility of the parents for the court-ordered support of others;
- Reasonable debts and liabilities of each child and parent; and
- Any other factors the court may deem relevant. (N.J.S.A. 2A:34-23)

In addition to these statutory factors, the Guidelines themselves specify the following additional specific factors a court may consider in making adjustments:

- equitable distribution of property in divorce,
- income tax consequences,
- fixed direct payments such as mortgage payments,

- a parent's unreimbursed medical or dental expenses,
- educational expenses for children,
- educational expenses required for a parent to improve earning capacity,
- the presence of more than six children in a single family household,
- special needs of gifted or disabled children,
- children's ages,
- any hidden costs of caring for children, including decreased income and career prospects, loss of saving, less time to shop economically,
- family units (i.e., one household) having more than six children,
- voluntary placement of children in foster care,
- a child's extraordinarily high income,
- pre-existing elder care obligations,
- tax consequences of health insurance payments, and
- multiple prior support obligations.
  (Appendix IX-A).

Some of these listed factors are discussed in more detail below. Parents must keep in mind that even this extensive list is not intended to be exclusive. If you are wondering whether a deviation would be appropriate in your case, consult Appendix IX-A directly, or contact a family law attorney for advice.

Extraordinary Supplemental Expenses:

In some situations, it is appropriate to add predictable and recurring expenses beyond health care or child-care needed for work to a child support order. Depending on the particular circumstances, such expenses may include private school tuition, expenses of special needs or gifted children, and transportation required for visitation. If parents disagree about the necessity of such expenses, a court will consider them in light of the child's best interests and the ability of both parents to pay. Factors a judge will consider in deciding whether to include private school tuition, for example, would include the quality of available public schools in the area and the child's prior educational setting.

- **Special Needs Children**. Children with physical, mental, or emotional disabilities are more likely than other children to have both predictable and unpredictable health care expenses exceeding $250 per year, as well as various types of extraordinary supplemental expenses. Some examples of health care expenses that a court might add to a child support award include unreimbursed fees for speech, occupational, or physical therapy, home health care, psychological counseling, prescription medications, prosthetics, and assistive technology. The necessity of any such expenses will be evaluated the same way as any other extraordinary expenses, with the court considering both the child's best interests and both parents' combined ability to pay the expense. Parents of special needs children need to be aware that receiving child support payments can affect a child's eligibility for "means-tested" government benefits, such as Supplemental Security Income (SSI) and Medicaid. A parent paying support may be able to minimize or eliminate this effect by depositing payments into a trust set up for the child's benefit rather than paying the other parent directly. A trust and estates attorney can provide more information on setting up a special needs trust.

- **Gifted Children.** The Guidelines specifically state that extraordinary expenses may also be justified for gifted children. A parent who wishes to claim such an expense will have to demonstrate that the child has a special gift or talent and that it is in the child's best interests to provide for the cost of nurturing the talent. This kind of extraordinary expense can cover a wide variety of goods and services, including special schooling, private tutoring, and assistive technology necessary to supplement the child's education.

Any non-recurring special expenses agreed upon or ordered by the court will generally be allocated in proportion to each parent's relative incomes. A parent can object to providing reimbursement for any expense that falls outside the scope of an order or agreement or is not supported by timely receipts.

Older Children:

Studies show that expenses are higher than average for teen-age children and lower than average for preteen children. The Guidelines ensure that support amounts that begin when children are young will even out over time, but if support begins after a child turns 12, a parent can request an adjustment based on higher costs. The standard age-related adjustment is 14.6%.

Payment of Post-Secondary Education Expenses:

New Jersey courts will sometimes order parents who can afford to do so to continue to contribute to the support of children between the ages of 18 and 24 who are pursuing post-high school education full-time. Minor children will have priority, and the Guidelines will not apply to children pursuing such education unless they are living at home and commuting to school.

New Jersey case law has established a list of factors, called the "Newburgh factors," that a court should consider, in addition to any other relevant factors, in determining whether or not to require a parent to contribute to a child's college expenses. These factors are:

- whether the parent, if still living with the child, would have contributed toward the costs of the requested higher education,

- the effect of the background, values and goals of the parent on the reasonableness of the expectation of the child for higher education,

- the amount of the contribution sought by the child for the cost of higher education,

- the ability of the parent to pay that cost,

- the relationship of the requested contribution to the kind of school or course of study sought by the child,

- the financial resources of both parents,

- the commitment to and aptitude of the child for the requested higher education,

- the financial resources of the child, including assets owned individually or held in custodianship or trust,

- the ability of the child to earn income during the school year or on vacation,

- the availability of financial aid in the form of college grants and loans,

- the child's relationship to the paying parent, including mutual affection and shared goals as well as responsiveness to parental advice and guidance, and

- the relationship of the education requested to any prior training and to the overall long-range goals of the child.

(Newburgh v. Arrigo, 88 N.J. 529, 545, 1982).

Both fathers and mothers need to be mindful that taking a dispute about college contributions to court could just end up eating into any funds that might instead be used for education. In a best-case scenario, parents will address the costs of higher education together early in a child's life and reach an agreement several years before such costs become a reality. High school-aged children should be involved in discussions about what kind of schooling parents can afford. Parents who disagree may want to consider mediation before filing a court case.

Extreme Income Situations:

- **Low Income.** The Guidelines include a "self-support reserve test" for parents with income at or near the current U.S. poverty guideline, to protect such parents from being left without any means of self-support.

- **High Income**. New Jersey public policy entitles children to share in the standard of living of both of their parents even if the parents are divorced and the higher income parent is no longer living with the child. In situations where parents have a combined annual net income—currently over $3,600 per week, or $187,200 per year—courts will begin by awarding the Appendix IX-F amount for the appropriate number of children based on a weekly income of $3,600, and will then add a discretionary amount based on the additional income after taking into account the factors (listed above) in the New Jersey Child Support Statute (N.J.S.A. 2A:34-23).

To calculate an appropriate amount, a parent who is expecting to receive additional discretionary child support payments should prepare two separate budgets, one for the parent and child together and one for the parent alone. The parent's budget for the children will include two parts, one based on the parent's own income and the other including additional items that children need to be able to share in the higher economic status of the parent paying support. Examples of items for which a court might approve payment of additional child support include:

138

- private school tuition,

- private tutoring,

- summer camps,

- music or art lessons,

- sports clinics,

- vacations,

- study abroad,

- a car for a child of driving age,

- payments on a family car,

- costs of maintaining the child's primary residence,

- extra clothing and incidental items for teenagers,

- a 529 plan for college funding, and

- additional savings accounts or trusts on behalf of the children.

Not every set of parents with combined net income in excess of $187,200 will be expected to pay for all of the listed items; nor is the list exclusive.

Agreements between Parents:

Parents can agree to an amount of child support that varies somewhat from the Guidelines, provided that the amount fulfills children's needs according to their best interests. A court will not approve a waiver of child support or an inappropriately low level of support.

Case Studies: Deviating from the Child support Guidelines

1. Payment of College Educational Expenses

Jack, a musician, and Diane, a physician, divorced 7 years ago after a fifteen-year marriage. At that time, they had two children, Katy, age 7, and Connor, age 10. After the divorce, Diane and Jack divided parenting time nearly equally, but Jack had slightly more time and was designated in the couple's Marital Settlement Agreement (MSA) as the Parent of Primary Residence. The MSA resolved all their immediate financial issues, including child support, but was silent on the issue of college contributions for the children. During the marriage, Jack and Diane had opened 529 education accounts for each child. The balance of Connor's account at the time of the divorce was about $18,000, while the balance of Katy's account was about $12,000. The parents agreed that any decisions regarding further contributions would be based on their actual financial circumstances as each child approached college age.

During Connor's senior year in high school, Diane earned about $170,000, while Jack earned about $60,000. Connor, who like his father was a talented and dedicated musician, was admitted to several schools, including the Mason Gross Conservatory at Rutgers University and a dual degree program at Oberlin College and Conservatory in Ohio. He had a GPA of 4.2, with a transcript that included a considerable number of Advanced Placement classes. Connor wished to attend Oberlin. He believed that the dual degree program was significantly more prestigious than any of his other options. It would also allow him to earn both a Bachelor of Arts and a Bachelor of Music in five years. He had received a scholarship from Oberlin consisting of a $5,000 per year contribution toward tuition over 5 years, for a total of $25,000. He had also received a scholarship from Rutgers in the amount of $10,000 total over 4 years.

Diane was willing to contribute a percentage share of Connor's total tuition based on her higher income, but she argued that the contribution should be capped at the amount of the Rutgers University tuition, rather than the substantially higher tuition at Oberlin. Jack brought a post-judgment motion to modify child support payments. His position was that Connor should be able to attend Oberlin because of the dedication he had shown and the combined ability of his parents to contribute to the costs of that school. He argued that each parent's contribution should be based on the total costs of attending Oberlin, including not only tuition, but also room, board, and other educational expenses.

After reviewing all the specific circumstances of the case and applying the factors listed in Newburgh v. Arrigo, 88 N.J. 529, 545, (1982), the judge ordered Connor's parents to contribute to his costs of attending Oberlin. Connor would be required to apply all available 529 and other education accounts, scholarships, loans, grants and any other forms of financial aid before either parent's obligation would come into play. After deducting funds from these sources, Diane would be responsible for paying 75% of the remaining educational expenses and Jack would be responsible for paying 25%. Educational expenses were to include tuition, room, board, books, fees, and reasonable costs of transportation to and from school. The court also ordered Diane to reimburse Jack for 75% of all application, admission and standardized test preparation course fees that he had paid for Connor.

Finally, the judge stated that in accordance with the current child support statute, the order would end when Connor either graduated from his program, withdrew from school, or turned 23 years old, whichever event occurred first in time.

2.   Extracurricular Expenses for a Gifted Child

Molly and Henry were married for 9 years and have been divorced for 7 years. They have one child together, 13-year-old Oliver. The parents share joint legal custody. Henry is designated as the Parent of Primary Residence, but Molly has nearly equal parenting time. Consistent with the New Jersey Child Support Guidelines, Molly pays Henry $162 in base child support every week, calculated on the Shared Parenting Worksheet. She has a gross income of approximately $48,000 a year, while Henry's gross income is approximately $35,000 a year.

A few years after their divorce, the parents had appeared in Family Court to resolve a parenting time dispute. Oliver, who was 11 years old at the time, was interviewed by the court. During the interview, he made it clear that his primary passion in life was snowboarding, and that he had been a rising star in the sport since he was a young child. He talked extensively about his eventual goal of competing in the Olympics. At the same time, he expressed a realistic attitude about the amount of hard work and dedication such a goal required. He was also aware of the financial burden on his parents and was already looking into how and when he might be able to start getting sponsorships.

Oliver's only major concern about parenting time had been the potential effect on his training and competition schedule. He stated that while his mother was supportive of his goals, his father seemed to have a better understanding of the total dedication required to be competitive at the top levels. Oliver put slightly more trust in Henry to help him get to the places he needed to be to succeed, and for this reason, he had said that if he had to choose, he would prefer to live primarily with Henry. In the parenting time decision, the judge stated that Oliver was one the most committed children he had ever interviewed, and that it was clear that snowboarding was not merely an extracurricular activity or hobby for Oliver, but rather an integral part of his current and future goals.

By age 13, Oliver's singular focus on training and competing had only sharpened. Henry asked Molly to pay half of all costs related to Oliver's snowboarding activities, including his equipment, clothing, coaching fees, competition entry fees and travel costs. Molly refused, arguing that the costs for such activities were already included in the basic child support obligation under New Jersey's Child Support Guidelines. She also argued that it would be unfair to simply order her to pay more, because she too often spent money directly on Oliver's snowboarding pursuits without requesting reimbursement from Henry.

Henry filed a court motion, claiming that he needs extra support because paying for the ordinary expenses relating to raising Oliver and providing shelter for him requires all of Henry's own modest income plus the $162 a week he currently receives in child support. It would be incredibly difficult, he argued, for him to shoulder all of Oliver's snowboarding expenses, which have been far in excess of normal for routine extracurricular activities, running well over $1,000 for the past year alone.

At a hearing on Henry's motion, the judge noted that although generally, a child's entertainment expenses are factored into a Guideline level support obligation, the

Guidelines also explicitly allow a court to order a supplemental payment to help cover costs related to the special needs and development of a "gifted" child. The judge emphasized that a clear distinction must be made between general extracurricular activities and an isolated discipline or skill in which a child has demonstrated a highly impressive commitment and for which additional support would clearly serve the child's best interest. The rationale behind including a gifted exception in the Guidelines, she continued, was not to reward a child or a primary parent with an arbitrary financial bonus for an inborn talent, but rather to provide an extra, reasonable, and specifically earmarked allowance for the purpose of promoting a child's extraordinary potential, when that child had demonstrated an unusually high ability and desire to succeed in a specific field.

Since the term "gifted" is not defined in the Guidelines, the judge observed, the question of whether or not any particular child is gifted must be left to the discretion of the courts on a case-by-case basis. She noted that the dictionary definition of "gifted" was "having exceptional talent or natural ability," and then went on to discuss the commonly understood nature of the term as generally referring to above-average skills and talents in athletics, academics, technology, the arts, or some other specific area. The judge found it notable that Oliver had so far enjoyed remarkable competitive success in his snowboarding endeavors, and also stated that it was important to consider his extraordinary desire, drive, focus, and commitment to succeed over the long term, as well as the fact that he had evidenced this unwavering commitment from a very young age. She further commented on Oliver's extraverted personality and his unusual poise and charisma, attributes that she felt were very likely to assist him in his future goals of obtaining sponsorships in his chosen pursuit.

Eventually, the judge concluded that in this case, it would be fair and equitable to deviate from the Guidelines and order both parents to contribute a small, reasonable annual amount to supplement and help support Oliver's snowboard-related expenses and efforts. After considering all available information, she ordered that unless the parents jointly agreed otherwise, each of them would be required to contribute a reasonable amount of up to an extra $500 per year, earmarked for the development of Oliver's snowboarding career. The judge urged the parents to collaborate about expenditures in advance whenever possible, to keep receipts of all direct expenditures, and to submit requests for contribution to the other parent promptly. Either parent would have thirty days after a request for reimbursement to submit their proportional contribution or challenge the appropriateness of the expense in writing.

Chapter 8

Obtaining and Enforcing Child Support Orders in New Jersey

If you and your child's other parent can agree on an amount for child support based on the New Jersey Child Support Guidelines as discussed above, you can sign and file a Consent Support Agreement and will not need to go to court. If you disagree on the appropriate amount of support, or if you have other issues to address, you will need to file an action in the Family Part of New Jersey Superior Court at your county courthouse. A child support case can be brought in New Jersey Superior Court as part of a divorce case or independently as a non-dissolution ("FD") matter.

In either case, the parent seeking support files and serves a complaint, along with several supporting documents. You can find more information about the appropriate forms and filing requirements from a family law attorney, or from the Self-Help Resource Center of the New Jersey Courts.

Filing in the Correct State

Before seeking a court order in New Jersey, you will need to ensure that you are filing in the right state. The New Jersey Child Support Guidelines apply only to cases within the jurisdiction of New Jersey state courts. Parents who do not live in New Jersey but have a child who does, as well as parents who do live in New Jersey but have a child who does not, need to determine whether New Jersey or another state has the right to issue and enforce child support orders. Laws sometimes differ substantially from state to state regarding support calculations, the age at which support payments end, and whether or not parents are responsible for contributing to a child's college education.

Jurisdiction in child support matters and parentage matters is determined by the Uniform Interstate Family Support Act (UIFSA) (N.J.S.A. 2A:4-30.65 et seq.). The UIFSA provides that a court making child support decisions must have personal jurisdiction over the parent responsible for paying support (the "obligor"). A state can obtain or retain personal jurisdiction over a parent responsible for paying child support under the following circumstances:

- The parent is personally served within a state with a summons or notice to appear in a court within that state,

- The parent voluntarily agrees to a particular court's jurisdiction,

- The parent lived with the child in the particular state at any point in the past,

- The parent lived in the state before the child's birth and provided prenatal expenses or support for the child,

- The child lives in the state as a result of acts or directives of the parent, or

- The child may have been conceived by the parent's engagement in sexual intercourse within the state.

To hear a new child support case, a court must have personal jurisdiction, not only over the parent responsible for paying support, but also over the other parent. If the child and both parents reside in the same state at the time of an initial application for child support, the court of that state will enter the order. If the child and both parents previously lived in the same state, but the paying parent has moved away, the original state will continue to have personal jurisdiction over the paying parent. If everyone has moved to new states, the parent seeking an order may have to obtain orders from the state where the paying parent now lives, by voluntarily submitting to that court's jurisdiction.

The state issuing the original orders will then keep jurisdiction to make any changes to orders, as long as at least one parent remains living in that state. Moving to another location within the state might change the county where the papers are filed, but it would not change which laws apply to the orders. If both parents leave the original state, there will be a reassessment of which court has jurisdiction over modifications.

As long as the court making decisions had legal authority to do so, the orders from that court are binding in every state. As with child custody jurisdiction under the UCCJEA, only one state or country can have exclusive and ongoing jurisdiction. Other state courts will recognize and enforce orders from the state with exclusive jurisdiction but will not modify such orders. When jurisdiction belongs to a foreign country, enforcement may depend on reciprocal agreements between states and countries. Without a reciprocal agreement, a state court can still decide that the law and procedures of the foreign country favor enforcement.

Jurisdictional disputes can be complicated. If you are trying to obtain child support orders in New Jersey and the other parent is trying to obtain them in another state or country, contact a family law attorney for advice.

Enforcing Child Support Payments

Making Payments and Keeping Records

The state agency responsible for helping parents obtain and enforce child support orders, including locating absent parents and establishing paternity, if necessary, is the Office of Child Support Services (OCSS) in the Division of Family Development of the New Jersey Department of Human Services (DHS). Parents can get a basic idea of the amount of child support a court might order by accessing the quick calculator available on the OCSS website. This calculator provides a very rough estimate only, however, and it is highly advisable to complete the appropriate worksheets and take into account all of the potential considerations discussed in this book and in the Child Support Guidelines themselves rather than relying on the quick calculator.

When a parent who has been ordered to pay child support receives a paycheck on a regular basis, income withholding (wage garnishment) will ensure payment. The New Jersey Family Support Payment Center (NJFSPC) receives and distributes payments. Parents not using wage garnishment can set up periodic payments through the NJFSPC, including on-line payments.

If you are making support payments directly to your child's other parent, be sure to document such payments. Note the amount of the payment, the date paid, the payment method and the purpose of the payment. If you make any cash payments, get a written receipt. Be very careful about purchasing extra things for your child if doing so would leave you unable to make your support payments. Many fathers love to buy things for their children, but are much less happy about turning money over to their former partner. While this is often understandable, the legal obligation must come first. If you are a non-custodial parent or a PPR, then in addition to making any agreed upon or court-ordered support payments, you are generally responsible for paying for things like food, transportation, and occasional entertainment for your child during your parenting time. Payment for things like clothing, personal care products or services, most entertainment and most miscellaneous items, however, is already included in your child support payments. Before buying things like this for your child, especially on a regular basis, ask the other parent to agree to reimburse you.

If you are the parent receiving support, keep records of all children's expenses that you believe the other parent should be paying for or contributing to, whether or not you are receiving such payment or contribution. Keep all of your documentation in a place that you will be able to locate easily in case you need to show it to your former spouse as a reminder or include it in an accounting for a future court date.

Fathers responsible for paying child support must understand that this is a serious legal obligation. If you are having difficulty keeping up payments due to job loss or another personal hardship, you should consult an attorney about making a request for a modification. Failing to do this could result in severe consequences, as further discussed below.

If you need help in reorganizing your finances so that you can pay both your support obligations and your other debts, consult with a credit counselor, a financial advisor, or an attorney to help you find options. Filing for bankruptcy may help you with other debts but it will not ameliorate your responsibility for paying support. Child support obligations take priority over many other types of debt and are not dischargeable in bankruptcy.

Collection and Enforcement of Awards by OCSS

The Office of Child Support Services records and monitors support due and paid through computerized records. The agency has several processes available to collect unpaid support and ensure that parents maintain medical insurance for children. The majority of the services offered by DHS are conducted through various county offices. OCSS works with the New Jersey Administrative Office of the Courts, county welfare agencies, county superior courts, and county probation divisions to provide comprehensive child support services. More information is available on the OCSS website. DHS maintains this interactive office locater tool to help people identify which office can provide specific services. You can also contact OCSS by telephone at: 1 (877) NJ KIDS 1.

Motions in Superior Court to Enforce Litigant's Rights

A parent who is not receiving timely child support can file a motion to enforce any financial obligation set forth in a signed parenting agreement or court order. A child support worker in the probation department can also file a motion to enforce litigants' rights on a parent's behalf. The superior court can order various remedies, as described in New Jersey Court Rules 1:10-3 and 5:3-7(b). These include the authority to order the responsible parent to bring all payments up to date, make future payments on time, and pay any attorney's fees the recipient has incurred in bringing the motion. They also include various tools available for ensuring compliance with orders for enforcement.

Child Support Enforcement tools include the following:

- Income Withholding. Arrears (overdue amounts), as well as regular payments, can be garnished through income withholding. The employer will receive a notice of the court-ordered amount, including any applicable arrears, deduct it directly from the parent's paycheck, and sends it to NJFSPC. The money is then distributed to the other parent. OCSS maintains a "New Hires Directory" to locate parents subject to child support orders and enforce payments. Employers in New Jersey are required to report new employees to the state within 20 days of hiring. The New Jersey Department of Labor can deduct support from unemployment or worker's compensation benefits payments as well.

- Seizures and Offsets. Past due child support payments can be collected through several different methods. These include seizing assets such as bank accounts, stocks, bonds, funds awarded in a civil suit or settlement, or lottery winnings of $600 or more. A federal tax refund may be withheld and applied to unpaid support if the past due amount is at least $500, or $150 in a public assistance case. New Jersey state tax refunds and homestead or saver rebates may be withheld to offset support payments that are one month or more in arrears. If the non-paying party is unemployed but has substantial assets, the support recipient can ask the court to record the past due support amount as a judgment and direct the sheriff to seize assets such as bank accounts, or liquidate and sell other assets to satisfy the judgment A recorded money judgment will also operate as a lien on any real estate the party owns.

- License Suspension. When a parent has not paid court-ordered child support for at least six months, a court may order any licensing agency to suspend or revoke that parent's driving, professional, occupational, recreational or sporting license, or deny a parent's outstanding application for such a license. Any warrant for arrest based on non-payment of child support also includes an automatic suspension of the subject's driver's license.

- Passport Denial. The U.S. State Department will deny an application for an initial or renewed passport to any parent who owes or has previously owed past-due child support of $2,500 or more. A parent can contest the denial by documenting that the arrears never exceeded $2,500, or that travel outside the country is necessary for employment, a serious medical emergency, or the imminent death of an immediate family member.

- Other Remedies. Back support in excess of $1,000 can be reported to credit agencies. If a parent fails to appear for a court date to establish paternity, set a support amount, or enforce payment of support—or disregards a court order relating to child support—the family court may issue a warrant for the parent's arrest. In the most serious cases, where a payer repeatedly disregards orders to bring payments up to date, a judge can issue a bench warrant for the party's arrest. This is a drastic remedy. Clearly, being in jail does not improve a party's ability to pay and may in fact make it considerably more difficult. Nevertheless, the threat of jail time does sometimes succeed in conveying the seriousness of the situation to a defaulting party when other methods have failed.

Case Studies: Obtaining and Enforcing Child Support Orders

This case shows how a court might handle collection of a large amount of past due child support:

Christine and Max were divorced 5 years ago. Their children, Carrie and Jesse, are currently 7 and 9 years old. Christine, who works up to 70 hours per week as a financial advisor, is by far the higher earning parent. Max is a graphic designer. Since Jesse's birth he has worked part-time as an independent contractor.

At the time of the divorce, the parents agreed that Max was much more able to serve as primary parent. They disagreed, however, on the appropriate amount of child support. Based on the income currently available to each parent, the court ordered Christine to pay $460 per week in child support directly to Max. Christine thought this was a ridiculous amount and objected to paying it. She did not, however, file an appeal of the order. Max not only believed that the order was fair, he suspected that Christine's current income could be even higher than she had reported, due to various raises and bonuses he thought she may have received. Nevertheless, he did not appeal the order either, believing that it would be sufficient to cover the children's needs.

To Max's surprise and discouragement, in spite of his repeated requests, Christine consistently failed to make the support payments. The amount of back support she owed gradually climbed to a total of $49,500. Max repeatedly asked her to become current with the payments, but she continued to ignore his requests. Eventually he felt he had no recourse other than to apply to the court for enforcement of the child support order.

The court found Christine to be in violation of her payment responsibility and ordered her to begin making timely and complete payments, as well as to begin bringing the accrued arrearage (past-due amount) up to date. A payment schedule required her to make a good faith down payment toward her existing arrearage in the lump sum of $10,000 within 14 days of the order, with another $25,000 due within the following 60 days, including $15,000 which the court ordered her to withdraw from her retirement account. Her anticipated tax refund in the amount of approximately $3,000 was also garnished to help satisfy the arrearage. To accommodate the arrearage that would still be outstanding after these payments, the court increased her weekly child support payments from $460 per week to $550 per week. Going forward, payments would be made through the appropriate probation department by means of wage garnishment.

Finally, the court placed Christine on a two-week bench warrant status. This meant that unless she made complete payments on time for two consecutive weeks, she could be arrested and incarcerated, with her release from jail conditional upon satisfaction of the payments. Max was somewhat surprised at the harshness of this last aspect of the order. He changed his mind, however, after his attorney, Leslie Barnes, explained to him that this kind of an order was fairly common with so called "deadbeat dads." Just because Christine is a mom," Ms. Barnes explained, "does not mean that she should be allowed to get away with treating child support so cavalierly."

Chapter 9

Modifying or Terminating Child Support

If you are paying support and believe that the amount is too high - or if you receiving support and believe that your children need more - you may be wondering what you need to do to make a change. Courts can make changes in child support payments whenever there is a substantial change in circumstances that is expected to continue indefinitely or for at least a considerable length of time. A change in the Child Support Guidelines is not a sufficient basis for review in and of itself. There must be independent support for a change in the individual case.

The initial burden of producing evidence of a substantial change in circumstances is on the parent seeking the modification. The court will look at the initial evidence and determine whether or not to hold a full hearing.

A court will not ordinarily address a change of circumstances claim until after the circumstances have actually occurred. Nevertheless, with some specific exceptions, once the new circumstances are in place, it is important to bring a claim promptly. People who wait months or even years before seeking a modification of child support will generally lose their opportunity to receive retroactive relief.

The following are some common reasons people bring motions requesting a change in child support payments:

- an increase or decrease in either parent's income,

- a change in a child's needs,

- a change in parenting time,

- the birth of a new child,

- a child's emancipation (achievement of financial independence), or

- a child's enrollment in college.

Increase or Decrease in Income:

A request for a decrease of child support payments must be based on a "good faith" (meaning not voluntary) decrease in ability to pay. An applicant will have to present documentation demonstrating a substantial and ongoing decrease in available income, including recent tax returns, and W-2 statements or business records showing decreased income.

If you are requesting a decrease in payments due to a job loss or pay-cut, you will need to provide the court with new financial statements as verification of income. You will also need to provide documentation supporting efforts to become re-employed at the former level, or evidence supporting a claim that such re-employment is not possible, such as an updated resume and a log demonstrating efforts to find work. The loss of income must actually occur prior to the request for a modification, and you will have to show that it is likely to continue on a long-term basis.

A parent receiving child support can generally request an increase for the same kinds of reasons that a paying parent could request a decrease. For example, a parent who has been laid off from a job can request an increase in the other parent's share of the support obligation if the lay-off is permanent and there is no comparable new position available. As with other requests for modification based on job loss or decreased income, the claim will require proof that the applicant is doing everything possible to become fully employed.

A parent whose income has decreased due to retirement will generally be able to obtain a decrease in child support payments as well; however, a court is unlikely to consider early retirement as a legitimate basis for reduction unless the parent has a very good reason for needing to retire and the modified child support will continue to be adequate for the child's needs. A request for modification based on a claim of disability must be based on sound medical testimony or evidence of an administrative determination of disability.

A request for a decrease in child support payments can also be based on a claim that the other parent's income has increased substantially, calling for a recalculation of the percentage share of support.

Change in a Child's Needs:

Children's needs often change over time. A child may develop trouble in school and require extra educational help, or demonstrate a special talent justifying lessons or attendance at enrichment programs or summer camp. Where the parents can both afford to pay for such things, a court might consider ordering the costs to be shared, even where one parent disagrees with the necessity.

Change in the Parenting Schedule:

A significant agreed upon change in the parenting schedule may call for a recalculation of support. A court will also recalculate support if one parent consistently fails to comply with the court-ordered schedule, and may also order that parent to pay the other parent's court costs and attorney's fees related to the recalculation.

Birth of Additional Children:

If one parent has additional natural or adopted children with a new partner after the court has set an initial support obligation, that parent can request that the child support obligation be recalculated to include the new child as a dependent. A court will not include stepchildren as dependents in the absence of some legal obligation to support them. A court that considers adjusting child support to allow for support of a new child will also consider the income of the new child's other parent and will impute income to that parent if appropriate. This type of recalculation would also be appropriate for adding a previously born child, if for some reason that child was not included in the original child support calculation.

A Child's Enrollment in College:

As previously discussed, in some cases, a New Jersey court will order a parent to contribute to a child's college or other post-secondary school expenses. When support orders are fixed while children are young, this contingency has rarely been taken into account, and if the parents cannot reach agreement on how to handle such expenses, a judge will intervene. The court will not order a continuation of support based on the Child Support Guidelines, but will instead consider what kind of support might be appropriate based on the individual circumstances of the case. (See "Payment of Post-Secondary Education Expenses," above.)

A Child's Emancipation:

Child support orders that do not contain a termination date will terminate automatically by the time a child turns 19, unless the custodial parent files an application for an extension before the child's 19th birthday (NJSA 2A:17-56.67). Paying parents can file an application before that time if they believe that the child is already "emancipated."

In New Jersey, emancipation occurs when a child goes "beyond the sphere of influence" of the parents and is no longer dependent on them for financial support. Courts often consider children who are between 18 and 23, and who are not employed full-time and are still attending school, including post high school programs, to be still within the sphere of parental influence. This is different from the law in the majority of states, but serves to aid young adults who remain dependent.

If a child support order is being administered by the Probation Division, both parents will be sent two written notices of proposed termination, the first at least 180 days prior to the child's 19th birthday and the second at least 90 days prior. The second notice will not be required if the custodial parent has already filed an application for extension, or if a new termination date has already been established. To the extent feasible, additional notices of termination will also be provided to parents by text or telephone message, or by other electronic means.

A custodial parent can seek continuation of support for a child past the age of 19 by establishing "sufficient proof," using court-approved forms and additional supporting documentation, of an acceptable reason for continuation. The request must specify a new projected future date for termination.

Acceptable reasons for continuation are:

- The child is still in high school;

- The child is enrolled full-time in a post-secondary program;

- The child has a mental or physical disability that existed prior to the child's 19th birthday; or

- Other exceptional circumstances subject to court approval.

A court approving a request for continuation will issue a new order with a specified prospective termination date, which must be on or before the child's 23rd birthday. The Child Support Guidelines are not automatically applicable to children who are over 18 and have graduated from high school. Instead the court will address the factors set out in the child support statute. (N.J.S.A. 2A:34-23).

Orders specifying unallocated child support for multiple children will not end automatically when the oldest child turns 19. Child support orders applicable to multiple children with amounts allocated per child will continue in effect minus the amount allocated to the child turning 19. In either situation, either parent can file a request for modification based on the change in status of the oldest child.

All New Jersey child support obligations end by operation of law when a child turns 23. While other forms of financial obligation may exist after a child reaches age 23, in no event will any such obligation be characterized as child support.

Before stopping court-ordered or agreed upon child support payments, speak to a New Jersey family law attorney about your specific situation.

Case Studies: Modifying and Terminating Child Support Orders

1.   Decrease in Supporting Parent's Income

Sam and Caroline divorced four years ago. They have two children together, 9-year-old Alice and 13-year-old Dustin. Sam was employed as a highly skilled machine operator until about four months ago when his job was fully automated and he was laid off. He had paid child support to Caroline without fail for three and a half years. Sam spent about two months looking for a new job before concluding that he would need some retraining. Last month, he accepted a job from a company that offered to pay for retraining, but also paid a much lower wage than his previous position.

Sam filed a request in family court for a reduction in his child support payments. He supplied the court with supporting documents, including the Case Information Statement from his divorce case; an updated Case Information Statement; paystubs and tax returns showing his income before the layoff; paystubs showing his current income; documentation supporting his explanation for the layoff; a current resume; and log cataloguing his efforts to become reemployed.

When Caroline also submitted an updated Case Information Statement, Sam was surprised to see that she was now making nearly twice the income she had been making four years ago. He then submitted completed child support guideline worksheets based on both his own decreased income and Caroline's increased income. The court granted Sam's request and his child support payments were dramatically reduced.

164

2.   Birth of an Additional Child

When Jessica and Paul divorced 4 years ago, they had two children, Ava, who is now 11 years old, and Charlie, who is now 8 years old. Under the terms of their Marital Settlement Agreement (MSA), Paul has paid child support to Jessica in the amount of $385 per week since the divorce.

Two years ago Paul married Chantel. Chantel came into the marriage with a child of her own, a 5-year-old girl named Lily. Lily's father had not paid child support for at least two years. After the marriage, Paul asked his attorney, Linda Green, if he could have his child support payments adjusted to include Lily as a third child, thereby lowering the amount he needed to pay Jessica for the children of his first marriage. Ms. Green told him that this was not likely to work, because he had no legal obligation to support Lily.

Last year, Chantel gave birth to Paul's 3rd child, Wesley. Paul again consulted Ms. Green, who gave him a different answer this time. On her advice, Paul applied to family court, requesting that his child support payments for Charlie and Ava be modified downward based on the "Other Dependent Deduction," which permits recalculation of support to add an additional legally dependent child. Paul supplied the court with supporting documents, including his MSA with Jessica, his Case Information Statement from the divorce case, an updated Case Information Statement, proof of current income, proof of Chantel's income, and completed child support guideline worksheets.

The court granted Paul's application and reduced his payments to Jessica for the support of Ava and Charlie, based on the fact that his income now needed to stretch further to accommodate the support of an additional child.

For More Information

At Weinberger Law Group all of our attorneys are engaged full time in the practice of family law. We are committed to providing honest recommendations and keeping the best interests of our clients and their children at the forefront at all times. Our attorneys will strive to resolve your matter out of court and will explore your settlement options, including New Jersey family mediation if appropriate in your case. When necessary, we will also fight vigorously to protect your rights.

You can find out more about our dedicated family law attorneys on our website, which is located at: www.WeinbergerLawGroup.com. Weinberger Divorce & Family Law Group offers an initial consultation with an experienced New Jersey Family Law Attorney at no cost.

Weinberger Divorce & Family Law Group has several office locations throughout New Jersey.

Weinberger Divorce & Family Law Group Headquarter Offices:
119 Cherry Hill Road, Suite 120
Parsippany, NJ 07054
Morris County

Tel: (888) 888-0919

Other Book Titles:
Weinberger Law Group Library Series
Of Family Law Guides

Contested Divorce

Uncontested Divorce

Child Support

Property Division

Alimony

Print books and ebook versions of the Weinberger
Law Group Library series can be ordered via Amazon or
by visiting www.WeinbergerLawGroup.com

Made in the USA
Middletown, DE
01 July 2023